CONTENTS

CONTENTS

THE TORTURE REPORT

ALSO BY SID JACOBSON AND ERNIE COLÓN

ANNE FRANK: THE ANNE FRANK HOUSE
AUTHORIZED GRAPHIC BIOGRAPHY
(2010)

VLAD THE IMPALER:
THE MAN WHO WAS DRACULA
(2009)

AFTER 9/11:
AMERICA'S WAR ON TERROR
(2008)

THE 9/11 REPORT:
A GRAPHIC ADAPTATION
(2006)

THE TORTURE REPORT

A GRAPHIC ADAPTATION

SID JACOBSON AND ERNIE COLÓN

NATION BOOKS, NEW YORK

Published by Nation Books, A Member of the Perseus Books Group
116 East 16th Street, 8th Floor
New York, NY 10003
Nation Books is a co-publishing venture of the Nation Institute and the Perseus Books Group
All rights reserved. Printed in the United States of America. No part of this book may be reproduced in any manner
whatsoever without written permission except in the case of brief quotations embodied in critical articles and reviews.
For information, address the Perseus Books Group, 250 West 57th Street, 15th Floor, New York, NY 10107. Books published
by Nation Books are available at special discounts for bulk purchases in the United States by corporations, institutions, and
other organizations. For more information, please contact the Special Markets Department at the Perseus Books Group,
2300 Chestnut Street, Suite 200, Philadelphia, PA 19103, or call (800) 810-4145, ext. 5000, or e-mail
special.markets@perseusbooks.com.

A CIP catalog record for this book is available from the Library of Congress.
ISBN: 978-1-56858-575-8 (HC)
ISBN: 978-1-56858-576-5 (EB)

10 9 8 7 6 5 4 3 2 1

INTRODUCTION
JANE MAYER

IN FEBRUARY 2009, one month after Barack Obama was sworn in as president, a secret meeting took place on Capitol Hill. Behind closed doors, in a soundproofed room, the members of the Senate's Select Committee on Intelligence gathered to hear a preliminary report on the previous administration's treatment of captured terrorism suspects.

For years George W. Bush and his top national security officials had assured Americans that while they had occasionally resorted to the use of what they called "Enhanced Interrogation Techniques," they had always treated terror suspects humanely, as American and international laws required. The United States was, after all, founded on the idea that no human being should be subjected to "cruel or unusual punishment." The United States had often led the world in writing and upholding the laws of war, which ban the degrading and inhumane treatment of captured prisoners. The country hadn't always lived up to its stated ideals, but these principles were the bedrock on which it was founded. What the senators heard during the meeting that day, however, utterly shocked them.

They learned that the Central Intelligence Agency had sanctioned brutal interrogations that were nothing short of nauseating. Instead of the safe, sophisticated, and carefully controlled techniques that the intelligence agency had described when seeking the senators' earlier approval, the report told the story of just one detainee, Abu Zubayda, who CIA officers had repeatedly slammed headlong into walls, crammed into a tiny box for hours on end, refused sleep for seventeen days, and waterboarded into unconsciousness numerous times. Despite the ordeal, he had yielded no useful intelligence. The only word to describe the CIA's treatment of this and other detainees, as President Obama later admitted, was "torture."

That meeting, in which U.S. senators got their first completely unvarnished glimpse of the true horror of the CIA's interrogation program, triggered one of the most extraordinary self-examinations ever undertaken by the U.S. government. The Senate Intelligence Committee, which by law is supposed to exercise oversight over the CIA, voted overwhelmingly to authorize the committee's staff to scour every scrap of evidence in order to get, and tell, the full, real, uncensored story of the CIA's interrogation program.

Six years later, what emerged from that effort is one of the most remarkable and successful truth-finding exercises ever undertaken by the U.S. Congress. A small handful of staff members on the Senate Intelligence Committee devoted years to culling through six million pages of CIA documents. The resulting report is a model of government accountability. So far only the 525-page summary of the full, final 6,770-page report has been publicly released, but it provides one of the most unsparing airings of misconduct, bungling, deception, and depravity by America's secret intelligence service ever to be shared with the American public.

The CIA had told Congress, the Justice Department, the White House, and the American public that it had only used harsh interrogation techniques on U.S.-held terror suspects sparingly, and that when it had, these controversial methods had resulted in intelligence breakthroughs that more than justified their use. As the Senate report shows, this was woefully untrue. Virtually nothing was learned from torturing detainees that couldn't have been found out through humane and legal methods.

By the time Obama was elected, a bipartisan consensus had formed that the CIA's brutal interrogation methods had gone too far, and must never be repeated. But by December 2014, when the report's summary was released, partisan warfare had grown much more pronounced, and shocking though it was in the twenty-first century, the issue of torture became just one more political football. Republicans on the Senate Intelligence Committee, after commissioning the report, denounced its findings. Former vice president Dick Cheney, who had been among the Bush administration's most ardent supporters of the CIA interrogation program, castigated it as "full of crap." The 2016 presidential campaign inflamed the issue even further as Donald Trump called for the return of waterboarding. Unlike the earlier proponents of harsh interrogation techniques, Trump dispensed with euphemisms and embraced torture outright, claiming that terror suspects would "talk a lot faster with torture."

Anyone who reads this horrifying report can see that such claims are bunk. The real facts are all here for every American to absorb. Some of the material is graphic, but this makes it a perfect subject for graphic depiction. Hopefully this new format will appeal to audiences of all ages and interests, including those who were previously unfamiliar with the story. The more who learn the truth, the better off the country will be, because there is no better safeguard against the revival of torture than a well-informed public.

WHO'S WHO

DICK CHENEY
U.S. VICE PRESIDENT,
2001–2009

GEORGE W. BUSH
U.S. PRESIDENT,
2001–2009

BARACK OBAMA
U.S. PRESIDENT, 2009–2016

DIANNE FEINSTEIN
CALIFORNIA SENATOR AND CHAIRMAN OF
THE U.S. SENATE SELECT COMMITTEE ON
INTELLIGENCE, 2009–2015

GEORGE TENET
CENTRAL INTELLIGENCE AGENCY (CIA) DIRECTOR

JOHN MCCAIN
ARIZONA SENATOR AND FORMER
PRESIDENTIAL CANDIDATE

ABU ZUBAYDAH
CIA DETAINEE

KHALID SHAYK MOHAMMAD (KSM)
CIA DETAINEE

ABU AHMED AL-KUWAITI
BIN LADEN FACILITATOR

USAMA BIN LADEN
HEAD OF AL-QA'IDA

HASSAN GHUL
CIA DETAINEE WHO GAVE
AT LEAST 21 INTELLIGENCE
REPORTS WITHOUT THE USE
OF EITS

JOSÉ PADILLA
AL-QA'IDA SUSPECT

JANAT GUL
CIA DETAINEE SUBJECTED TO
ENHANCED INTERROGATION
TECHNIQUES (EITS)

FOREWORD

THE U.S. SENATE SELECT COMMITTEE ON INTELLIGENCE (SSCI) ISSUED THE *COMMITTEE STUDY OF THE CENTRAL INTELLIGENCE AGENCY'S DETENTION AND INTERROGATION PROGRAM*, ITS HIGHLY DAMAGING INDICTMENT OF THE CENTRAL INTELLIGENCE AGENCY'S (CIA) DETENTION AND INTERROGATION PROGRAM FOR ITS SECRET USE OF TORTURE, OTHER HARSH INTERROGATION TACTICS, AND SEVERE CONFINEMENT PROTOCOLS, ON TUESDAY, SEPTEMBER 9, 2014. THE BUSH ADMINISTRATION AND MANY REPUBLICAN PARTY MEMBERS HAVE VOCIFEROUSLY PROTESTED THE COMMITTEE'S FINDINGS.

SENATOR DIANNE FEINSTEIN OF CALIFORNIA, CHAIRMAN OF THE SSCI, CALLED THE CIA PROGRAM "A STAIN ON OUR VALUES AND OUR HISTORY . . ."

-1-

IN THE FOREWORD TO THE REPORT, CHAIRMAN DIANNE FEINSTEIN POINTS OUT THAT THE HORRORS OF 9/11, STILL VIVID TODAY, SET THE STAGE FOR THE CIA'S ACTIONS.

"NEVERTHELESS," SHE CONTINUES, "SUCH PRESSURE, FEAR, AND EXPECTATION OF FURTHER TERRORIST PLOTS DO NOT JUSTIFY, TEMPER, OR EXCUSE IMPROPER ACTIONS TAKEN BY INDIVIDUALS OR ORGANIZATIONS IN THE NAME OF NATIONAL SECURITY."

FEINSTEIN CONCLUDES WITH THE HOPE THAT . . .

NO, GENTLEMEN, *NO!* IT IS WRONG AND, WHAT'S MORE, *IT DOESN'T **WORK!***

"U.S. POLICY WILL NEVER AGAIN ALLOW FOR SECRET INDEFINITE DETENTION AND THE USE OF COERCIVE INTERROGATIONS . . . WE CANNOT AGAIN ALLOW HISTORY TO BE FORGOTTEN AND GRIEVOUS PAST MISTAKES TO BE REPEATED."

COMMITTEE'S FINDINGS AND CONCLUSIONS

1. THE CIA'S ENHANCED INTERROGATION TECHNIQUES (EITS) WERE NOT AN EFFECTIVE MEANS OF GAINING INTELLIGENCE OR COOPERATION.

SEVEN OF THIRTY-NINE CAPTIVES SUBJECTED TO EITS PRODUCED NO INTELLIGENCE INFORMATION. OTHERS PROVIDED IMPORTANT INTELLIGENCE WITHOUT BEING SUBJECTED TO THE TECHNIQUES. MANY PRISONERS PROVIDED FABRICATED INFORMATION WHEN SUBJECTED TO THE TECHNIQUES.

2. THE CIA'S JUSTIFICATION FOR THE USE OF EITS RESTED ON INACCURATE CLAIMS OF THEIR EFFECTIVENESS.

THE SENATE COMMITTEE REVIEWED 20 PURPORTED SUCCESSES AND FOUND THEM TO BE INACCURATE IN FUNDAMENTAL ASPECTS.

3. THE INTERROGATIONS OF CIA DETAINEES WERE BRUTAL AND FAR WORSE THAN THE CIA REPRESENTED.

STARTING WITH THEIR FIRST DETAINEE, ABU ZUBAYDAH, THE CIA APPLIED EITS FOR UP TO WEEKS AT A TIME, USING WATERBOARDING, SLAPS, AND WALLINGS (SLAMMING DETAINEES AGAINST A WALL), IN COMBINATION WITH SLEEP DEPRIVATION AND NUDITY.

4. THE CONDITIONS OF CONFINEMENT FOR CIA DETAINEES WERE HARSHER THAN THE CIA REPRESENTED.

COBALT [A CIA DETENTION FACILITY]

WAS A VIRTUAL DUNGEON, COLD AS HELL AND LOUD AS ANY EAR COULD TAKE!

IT WAS ITSELF AN ENHANCED INTERROGATION TECHNIQUE.

WHEN . . . WHEN WILL TH–THIS STOP?

WHEN YOU TELL US WHAT WE NEED TO KNOW!

I KNOW IT'S OVER NOW! I WALKED WITH OUR SAVIOR LAST NIGHT. YES, HE WAS WELCOMING ME INTO HEAVEN!

MULTIPLE DETAINEES WHO HAD BEEN SUBJECTED TO EITS SUFFERED FROM HALLUCINATIONS, PARANOIA, INSOMNIA, AND ATTEMPTS AT SELF-MUTILATION.

PRISONERS WERE WALKED AROUND NAKED FOR LONG, LONG HOURS WHILE OTHERS HAD THEIR HANDS SHACKLED TO THE CEILING FOR DAYS.

YOU WANT MY BLOOD? I'LL GIVE YOU MY BLOOD!

5. THE CIA REPEATEDLY PROVIDED INACCURATE INFORMATION TO THE DEPARTMENT OF JUSTICE, IMPEDING A PROPER LEGAL ANALYSIS OF THE PROGRAM

6. THE CIA HAS ACTIVELY AVOIDED OR IMPEDED CONGRESSIONAL OVERSIGHT OF THE PROGRAM, INCLUDING PROVIDING INACCURATE INFORMATION TO THE SSCI.

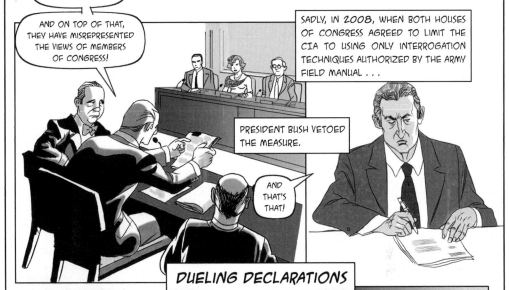

THERE ARE NUMEROUS INACCURACIES HERE!

AND ON TOP OF THAT, THEY HAVE MISREPRESENTED THE VIEWS OF MEMBERS OF CONGRESS!

SADLY, IN 2008, WHEN BOTH HOUSES OF CONGRESS AGREED TO LIMIT THE CIA TO USING ONLY INTERROGATION TECHNIQUES AUTHORIZED BY THE ARMY FIELD MANUAL . . .

PRESIDENT BUSH VETOED THE MEASURE.

AND THAT'S THAT!

DUELING DECLARATIONS

CIA DIRECTOR JOHN O. BRENNAN

THE OVERWHELMING MAJORITY OF OFFICERS INVOLVED IN THE PROGRAM CARRIED OUT THEIR RESPONSIBILITIES FAITHFULLY AND IN ACCORDANCE WITH THE LEGAL AND POLICY GUIDANCE THEY WERE PROVIDED.

VICE PRESIDENT DICK CHENEY

I THINK THAT'S ALL A BUNCH OF HOOEY! THE AGENCY DID NOT WANT TO PROCEED WITHOUT AUTHORIZATION, AND IT WAS ALSO REVIEWED LEGALLY BY THE JUSTICE DEPARTMENT BEFORE THEY UNDERTOOK THE PROGRAM.

I HAVE OFTEN SAID . . . THAT THIS QUESTION IS NOT ABOUT OUR ENEMIES; IT'S ABOUT US. IT'S ABOUT WHO WE ARE . . . AND WHO WE ASPIRE TO BE.

SENATOR JOHN MCCAIN

7. THE CIA IMPEDED WHITE HOUSE OVERSIGHT AND DECISION-MAKING.

AND NO ONE DARED DIVULGE A THING TO SECRETARY POWELL OR DEPUTY SECRETARY ARMITAGE.

IT'S SEPTEMBER 2003, AND WE JUST LEARNED ABOUT THEIR DAMN SO-CALLED EITS!

SIR, THEY'VE ONCE AGAIN DENIED FBI ACCESS TO THE DETAINEES.

8. THE CIA'S OPERATION AND MANAGEMENT OF THE PROGRAM COMPLICATED, AND IN SOME CASES IMPEDED, THE NATIONAL SECURITY MISSIONS OF OTHER EXECUTIVE BRANCH AGENCIES.

BUT DIRECTOR MUELLER HAS SPECIFICALLY ASKED FOR IT!

9. THE CIA IMPEDED OVERSIGHT BY THE CIA'S OFFICE OF INSPECTOR GENERAL (OIG).

THEY GAVE THE OIG INACCURATE INFORMATION AND, IN 2007, WENT SO FAR AS TO ORDER AN UNPRECEDENTED REVIEW OF THE OIG ITSELF IN RESPONSE TO ITS INQUIRIES INTO THE PROGRAM.

10. THE CIA COORDINATED THE RELEASE OF CLASSIFIED INFORMATION TO THE MEDIA, INCLUDING INACCURATE INFORMATION CONCERNING THE EFFECTIVENESS OF EITS.

YOU'RE GOING TO DO THAT TO ME?

11. THE CIA WAS UNPREPARED AS IT BEGAN OPERATING ITS DETENTION AND INTERROGATION PROGRAM MORE THAN SIX MONTHS AFTER BEING GRANTED DETENTION AUTHORITIES.

THE CAPTURE OF ABU ZUBAYDAH, A SAUDI CITIZEN ACCUSED OF PLOTTING THE 9/11 ATTACKS AND HEADING A TRAINING CAMP FOR AL-QA'IDA RECRUITS, IN MARCH 2002 PROMPTED THE CIA TO CONSIDER VARIOUS DETENTION OPTIONS. STARTING IN AUGUST OF THAT YEAR, HE BECAME THE FIRST PRISONER TO UNDERGO EITS.

IN PART TO AVOID DECLARING ZUBAYDAH'S CAPTURE TO THE INTERNATIONAL COMMITTEE OF THE RED CROSS, WHICH WOULD BE REQUIRED IF HE WAS HELD ON A U.S. MILITARY BASE, THE CIA SOUGHT THE PRESIDENT'S APPROVAL TO SEND HIM TO AN UNNAMED BASE, AND RECEIVED IT!

GOOD WORK, MR. PRESIDENT!

HOLY SHIT! WE'RE GOING TO DO THAT?

THE CIA ADAPTED NEW INTERROGATION METHODS FROM THE TRAINING PROGRAM AT THE U.S. AIR FORCE SURVIVAL, EVASION, RESISTANCE, AND ESCAPE (SERE) SCHOOL, DESIGNED TO PREPARE MILITARY PERSONNEL FOR THE TORTUROUS TREATMENTS THEY MAY FACE IF CAPTURED BY AN ENEMY THAT DID NOT ADHERE TO THE GENEVA CONVENTIONS. YES, THESE WERE METHODS THE *ENEMY* MIGHT USE.

12. THE CIA'S MANAGEMENT AND OPERATION OF ITS DETENTION AND INTERROGATION PROGRAM WAS DEEPLY FLAWED THROUGHOUT THE PROGRAM'S DURATION, PARTICULARLY IN 2002 AND EARLY 2003.

THE CIA'S *COBALT* DETENTION FACILITY IN [COUNTRY REDACTED] BEGAN OPERATIONS IN SEPTEMBER 2002 AND HOUSED MORE THAN HALF OF THE 119 DETAINEES IDENTIFIED IN THIS STUDY. FEW FORMAL RECORDS OF THE DETAINEES WERE KEPT AND UNTRAINED CIA OFFICERS WERE OFTEN IN CHARGE, USING HARSH TECHNIQUES THAT WOULD NEVER BECOME PART OF THE "ENHANCED" PROGRAM. THE CIA OFFICERS' INABILITY TO SPEAK THE PRISONER'S LANGUAGE WAS AN "ONGOING PROBLEM."

BUT, SIR, YOU HAVEN'T FED US FOR DAYS.

THEN EAT YOUR HEART OUT! HAH!

AS FAR AS I'M CONCERNED, HE BROUGHT IT ON HIMSELF!

IF YOU DON'T UNDERSTAND MY LANGUAGE, PERHAPS YOU'LL UNDERSTAND MY FISTS!

IN NOVEMBER 2002, A DETAINEE WHO HAD BEEN PRACTICALLY NUDE AND CHAINED TO THE CONCRETE FLOOR DIED FROM SUSPECTED HYPOTHERMIA.

NUMEROUS CIA OFFICERS HAD SERIOUS DOCUMENTED PERSONAL AND PROFESSIONAL PROBLEMS, INCLUDING HISTORIES OF VIOLENCE AND RECORDS OF ABUSIVE TREATMENT OF OTHERS.

DON'T LET HIM MAKE ME LOSE MY COOL . . . DON'T LET HIM.

13. TWO CONTRACT PSYCHOLOGISTS—NEITHER EXPERIENCED AS INTERROGATORS OR HAVING ANY SPECIAL KNOWLEDGE OF AL-QA'IDA, TERRORISM, OR RELEVANT CULTURAL OR LINGUAL EXPERIENCE—DEVISED THE CIA'S EITS AND PLAYED A CENTRAL ROLE IN THE OPERATION, ASSESSMENTS, AND MANAGEMENT OF THE CIA'S DETENTION AND INTERROGATION PROGRAM.

IN 2005, THE PSYCHOLOGISTS FORMED THEIR OWN COMPANY, AND SHORTLY AFTER THAT THE CIA OUT-SOURCED VIRTUALLY ALL ASPECTS OF THE PROGRAM.

IN 2006, THE VALUE OF THE CIA'S BASE CONTRACT WITH THE NEW COMPANY WAS IN EXCESS OF $180 MILLION.

14. PRIOR TO 2004, CIA DETAINEES WERE SUBJECTED TO COERCIVE INTERROGATION TECHNIQUES THAT HAD NOT BEEN APPROVED BY THE DEPARTMENT OF JUSTICE OR HAD NOT BEEN AUTHORIZED BY CIA HEADQUARTERS, SUCH AS NUDITY, DIETARY MANIPULATION, ABDOMINAL SLAPS, AND COLD-WATER DOUSING.

THERE WERE LESS THAN A HUNDRED DETAINED, AND LESS THAN A THIRD OF THEM WERE SUBJECTED TO UH . . . EITS.

15. THE CIA NEVER CONDUCTED A COMPREHENSIVE AUDIT NOR DEVELOPED A COMPLETE AND ACCURATE LIST OF THOSE DETAINED OR SUBJECTED TO EITS. THE COMMITTEE'S REVIEW OF THEIR RECORDS SHOWED AT LEAST 119 WERE DETAINED AND AT LEAST 39 WERE SUBJECTED TO EITS. THIS MAY ALSO BE TOO LOW, AS SOME RECORDS THAT SHOULD HAVE BEEN KEPT WERE NOT.

WELL, HE'S ASKING US TO DO IT AGAIN.

PUT IT WITH THE REST OF THEM. IN THE FILE.

16. THE CIA NEVER CONDUCTED A CREDIBLE ANALYSIS OF THE EFFECTIVENESS OF ITS INTERROGATION PROGRAM DESPITE RECOMMENDATIONS FROM ITS INSPECTOR GENERAL.

DID YOU HEAR WHAT I SAID HE DID, SIR?

I DID, AND YOU DID YOUR JOB, TYLER!

AND I TELL YOU, SIR, THAT THE DETAINEE IS *NOT* WITHHOLDING ANY INFORMATION!

17. THE CIA RARELY REPRIMANDED OR HELD PERSONNEL ACCOUNTABLE FOR SERIOUS VIOLATIONS, INAPPROPRIATE ACTIVITIES, AND MANAGEMENT FAILURES.

18. THE CIA MARGINALIZED AND IGNORED NUMEROUS INTERNAL CRITICISMS AND OBJECTIONS CONCERNING THE OPERATION AND MANAGEMENT OF ITS DETENTION AND INTERROGATION PROGRAM.

THIS INCLUDED CONCERNS ABOUT THE EITS PROGRAM EXPRESSED BY CIA AND MEDICAL OFFICERS, WHO DISAGREED WITH THE USE OF THE TECHNIQUES AGAINST DETAINEES THEY HAD DETERMINED WERE *NOT* WITHHOLDING INFORMATION.

19. THE CIA INTERROGATION PROGRAM WAS INHERENTLY UNSUSTAINABLE.

IT EFFECTIVELY ENDED BY 2006 DUE TO UNAUTHORIZED PRESS DISCLOSURES, REDUCED COOPERATION FROM OTHER NATIONS, AND LEGAL AND OVERSIGHT CONCERNS. PRESIDENT BUSH PUBLICLY DISCLOSED THE PROGRAM ON SEPTEMBER 6, 2006, AND ON SEPTEMBER 29, HE SAID . . .

SUSPECTED TERRORISTS PROVIDED INFORMATION THAT HELPED US PROTECT THE AMERICAN PEOPLE!

ON JULY 20, 2007, BUSH SIGNED EXE-CUTIVE ORDER 13440, BANNING TORTURE OF CAPTIVES BY ALL INTELLIGENCE OFFICES.

20. THE CIA'S DETENTION AND INTERROGATION PROGRAM DAMAGED THE UNITED STATES' STANDING IN THE WORLD AND RESULTED IN OTHER SIGNIFICANT MONETARY AND NON-MONETARY COSTS.

I'M SURE YOU CAN FIND A WAY TO ALLOW US TO BUILD HERE.

THE PROGRAM CAUSED IMMEASURABLE DAMAGE TO THE UNITED STATES' LONG-STANDING GLOBAL LEADERSHIP ON HUMAN RIGHTS IN GENERAL AND THE PREVENTION OF TORTURE IN PARTICULAR.

CIA RECORDS INDICATE THAT THE PROGRAM COST WELL OVER $300 MILLION IN NON-PERSONNEL COSTS. AND TO ENCOURAGE GOVERNMENTS TO CLANDESTINELY HOST CIA DETENTION SITES, THE AGENCY PROVIDED MILLIONS IN CASH PAYMENTS TO FOREIGN GOVERNMENT OFFICIALS AND AGENTS WERE URGED TO "THINK BIG" IN TERMS OF THAT ASSISTANCE.

EXECUTIVE SUMMARY: BACKGROUND ON COMMITTEE STUDY

ON DECEMBER 11, 2007, THE SSCI INITIATED A REVIEW OF THE DESTRUCTION OF VIDEOTAPES RELATED TO THE INTERROGATION OF CIA DETAINEES ABU ZUBAYDAH AND ABD AL-RAHIM AL-NASHIRI. THIS ULTIMATELY LED TO A BROADER REVIEW OF THE CIA'S DETENTION AND INTER-ROGATION PROGRAM. ON MARCH 5, 2009, THE SSCI APPROVED THE STUDY.

THE SSCI'S STUDY IS THE MOST COMPREHENSIVE REVIEW EVER CONDUCTED OF THE CIA'S DETENTION AND INTERROGATION PROGRAM. THE CIA PROVIDED THE SSCI WITH ALL CIA RECORDS RELATED TO THE PROGRAM, AN AMOUNT OF MORE THAN SIX MILLION PAGES. THE STUDY IS BASED PRINCIPALLY ON A REVIEW OF THOSE PAGES.

THROUGHOUT THE REPORT, NON-SUPERVISORY CIA PERSONNEL ARE LISTED BY PSEUDONYMS. THE COUNTRIES WHERE CIA DETENTION FACILITIES WERE LOCATED WERE ALSO OBFUSCATED, COUNTRY 1, COUNTRY 2, ETCETERA. THE CIA ALSO REQUESTED THAT THE SSCI REPLACE THE ORIGINAL CODE NAMES FOR CIA DETENTION SITES WITH NEW NAMES.

OVERALL HISTORY AND OPERATION OF THE CIA'S DETENTION AND INTERROGATION PROGRAM

ON SEPTEMBER 17, 2001, SIX DAYS AFTER THE 9/11 ATTACKS, PRESIDENT GEORGE W. BUSH SIGNED A COVERT ACTION MEMORANDUM OF NOTIFICATION (MON) AUTHORIZING THE DIRECTOR OF THE CIA TO UNDERTAKE OPERATIONS TO CAPTURE AND DETAIN PERSONS POSING THREATS OF VIOLENCE OR DEATH TO U.S. PERSONS OR INTERESTS OR PLANNING TERRORIST ACTIVITIES.

JUST THREE DAYS BEFORE, ON SEPTEMBER 14, THE CIA CHIEF OF OPERATIONS OF [REDACTED] SENT E-MAILS TO CIA STATIONS SEEKING SUGGESTIONS ON LOCATIONS FOR CIA DETENTION FACILITIES.

ON SEPTEMBER 27, CIA HEADQUARTERS INFORMED CIA STATIONS THAT CIA DETENTION FACILITIES WOULD HAVE TO MEET U.S. POW STANDARDS.

THIS WAS FOLLOWED IN NOVEMBER BY CIA HEADQUARTERS DECLARING THAT THESE DETENTION AND INTERROGATION SITES SHOULD "MEET THE REQUIREMENTS OF U.S. LAW AND THE FEDERAL RULES OF CRIMINAL PROCEDURE."

AT THAT TIME, THE CIA HAD IN PLACE LONG-STANDING STANDARDS FOR CONDUCTING INTERROGATIONS: "INHUMANE PHYSICAL OR PSYCHOLOGICAL TECHNIQUES ARE COUNTERPRODUCTIVE BECAUSE THEY DO NOT PRODUCE INTELLIGENCE AND WILL PROBABLY RESULT IN FALSE ANSWERS."

A CIA HANDBOOK FROM OCTOBER 2001 DECLARES: "IT IS CIA POLICY TO NEITHER PARTICIPATE DIRECTLY IN NOR ENCOURAGE INTERROGATION WHICH INVOLVES THE USE OF FORCE, MENTAL OR PHYSICAL TORTURE, EXTREMELY DEMEANING INDIGNITIES, OR EXPOSURE TO INHUMANE TREATMENT OF ANY KIND AS AN AID TO INTERROGATION."

HOWEVER, ON FEBRUARY 7, 2002, PRESIDENT BUSH ISSUED A MEMORANDUM STATING...

... THAT NEITHER AL-QA'IDA NOR TALIBAN DETAINEES QUALIFIED AS PRISONERS OF WAR REQUIRING HUMANE TREATMENT OF INDIVIDUALS IN A CONFLICT.

JUST IN TIME FOR THE CAPTURE OF ABU ZUBAYDAH IN LATE MARCH 2002. THE AL-QA'IDA FACILITATOR WAS WOUNDED AND CAPTURED IN A RAID BY PAKISTANI FORCES AND THE CIA.

HE SAYS, "I CAN ONLY TELL YOU WHAT I KNOW."

ZUBAYDAH WAS ASSESSED BY THE CIA TO POSSESS DETAILED KNOWLEDGE OF AL-QA'IDA'S TERRORIST PLANS, BUT THE SENATE COMMITTEE LATER DETERMINED THIS WAS SIGNIFICANTLY OVERSTATED.

YES, THIS WILL BE YOUR HOME FOR A *LONG* WHILE.

AFTER MUCH DELIBERATION, ZUBAYDAH WAS PLACED AT A COVERT DETENTION FACILITY IN [REDACTED]. KNOWN AS *DETENTION SITE GREEN*, IT WAS THE LAST CIA DETENTION FACILITY KNOWN TO THE PRESIDENT AND THE VICE PRESIDENT--A WHITE HOUSE POLICY TO AVOID INADVERTENT DISCLOSURES OF THE LOCATIONS OF CIA DETENTION SITES.

EARLY IN HIS STAY, FBI SPECIAL AGENTS, WITH THE ADVANTAGE OF SPEAKING ARABIC, JOINED THE CIA IN QUESTIONING ABU ZUBAYDAH. THE DETAINEE TOLD THE FBI OFFICERS HE WANTED TO COOPERATE AND PROVIDE BACKGROUND INFORMATION ON HIS ACTIVITIES.

HE SAYS, HE BELIEVES HE KNOWS WHO YOU'RE LOOKING FOR.

BUT HIS MEDICAL CONDITION DETERIORATED AND HE REQUIRED IMMEDIATE HOSPITALIZATION.

WHILE HE WAS AT THE HOSPITAL, HE CONTINUED TO PROVIDE INFORMATION TO THE CIA AND THE FBI WITH THE USE OF AN ARABIC ALPHABET CHART.

THE FBI OFFICERS NEVER LEFT HIS SIDE, EVEN ASSISTING IN HIS MEDICAL CARE.

HIM! HIM! HIM!

DURING AN APRIL 10, 2002, DEBRIEFING SESSION IN THE HOSPITAL, ZUBAYDAH REVEALED TO FBI OFFICERS THAT A PERSON NAMED "MUKHTAR" WAS THE MASTERMIND OF THE 9/11 ATTACKS. HE IDENTIFIED "MUKHTAR" AS KHALID SHAYK MOHAMMAD (KSM).

KSM HAD BEEN INDICTED IN 1996 FOR HIS ROLE IN AN ATTEMPT TO DETONATE EXPLOSIVES MIDFLIGHT ON 12 U.S. AIRCRAFT.

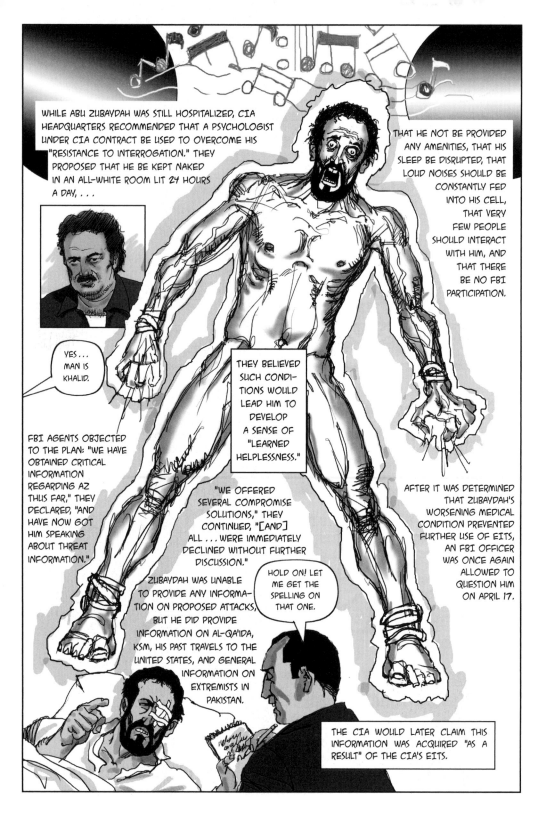

WHILE ABU ZUBAYDAH WAS STILL HOSPITALIZED, CIA HEADQUARTERS RECOMMENDED THAT A PSYCHOLOGIST UNDER CIA CONTRACT BE USED TO OVERCOME HIS "RESISTANCE TO INTERROGATION." THEY PROPOSED THAT HE BE KEPT NAKED IN AN ALL-WHITE ROOM LIT 24 HOURS A DAY, . . .

THAT HE NOT BE PROVIDED ANY AMENITIES, THAT HIS SLEEP BE DISRUPTED, THAT LOUD NOISES SHOULD BE CONSTANTLY FED INTO HIS CELL, THAT VERY FEW PEOPLE SHOULD INTERACT WITH HIM, AND THAT THERE BE NO FBI PARTICIPATION.

YES . . . MAN IS KHALID.

THEY BELIEVED SUCH CONDI-TIONS WOULD LEAD HIM TO DEVELOP A SENSE OF "LEARNED HELPLESSNESS."

FBI AGENTS OBJECTED TO THE PLAN: "WE HAVE OBTAINED CRITICAL INFORMATION REGARDING AZ THUS FAR," THEY DECLARED, "AND HAVE NOW GOT HIM SPEAKING ABOUT THREAT INFORMATION."

"WE OFFERED SEVERAL COMPROMISE SOLUTIONS," THEY CONTINUED, "[AND] ALL . . . WERE IMMEDIATELY DECLINED WITHOUT FURTHER DISCUSSION."

AFTER IT WAS DETERMINED THAT ZUBAYDAH'S WORSENING MEDICAL CONDITION PREVENTED FURTHER USE OF EITS, AN FBI OFFICER WAS ONCE AGAIN ALLOWED TO QUESTION HIM ON APRIL 17.

ZUBAYDAH WAS UNABLE TO PROVIDE ANY INFORMA-TION ON PROPOSED ATTACKS, BUT HE DID PROVIDE INFORMATION ON AL-QA'IDA, KSM, HIS PAST TRAVELS TO THE UNITED STATES, AND GENERAL INFORMATION ON EXTREMISTS IN PAKISTAN.

HOLD ON! LET ME GET THE SPELLING ON THAT ONE.

THE CIA WOULD LATER CLAIM THIS INFORMATION WAS ACQUIRED "AS A RESULT" OF THE CIA'S EITS.

I DON'T KNOW IF HE NEEDS A REST, BUT I SURE DO!

IN EARLY JUNE 2002, THE CIA RECOMMENDED THAT ABU ZUBAYDAH SPEND SEVERAL WEEKS IN ISOLATION WHILE THE TEAM MEMBERS DEPARTED THE FACILITY AS A MEANS OF KEEPING THE DETAINEE "OFF-BALANCE" AND TO ALLOW THE TEAM NEEDED TIME OFF.

AND TO DISCUSS THE "ENDGAME" FOR THE DETAINEE.

YOU GUYS ARE DOING AN AWFUL LOT OF QUESTIONING OF SOMEONE LYING ALONE IN A SEALED ROOM.

DESPITE THE FACT THAT THE DETAINEE WAS IN ISOLATION FOR 47 DAYS, FROM JUNE 18 TO AUGUST 4, 2002, THE CIA DISSEMINATED 37 INTELLIGENCE REPORTS BASED ON SUPPOSED INTERROGATIONS OF ZUBAYDAH IN JUNE 2002.

LATER, THE CIA PUBLICLY REPORTED THAT DURING THE MONTH OF JUNE THE DETAINEE "STOPPED ALL COOPERATION" WITH THE CIA.

BUT PRIOR TO ZUBAYDAH'S 47-DAY ISOLATION PERIOD, THE DETAINEE PROVIDED INFORMATION ON AL-QA'IDA ACTIVITIES, ATROCITIES, PLANS, CAPABILITIES, AND RELATIONSHIPS AS WELL AS ITS LEADERSHIP, STRUCTURE, DECISION-MAKING PROCESS, TRAINING, AND TACTICS. ALL WITHOUT THE USE OF EITS.

HE KNOWS TOO DAMN MUCH NOT TO KNOW OF A PLANNED ATTACK.

THERE'S ONLY ONE WAY TO GET IT OUT OF HIM!

HIS INABILITY TO PROVIDE INFORMATION ON THEIR NEXT ATTACK IN THE UNITED STATES SERVED AS THE BASIS OF THE CIA'S BELIEF THAT HE REQUIRED THE USE OF EITS.

THE CIA LATER CONCLUDED THAT THIS WAS INFORMATION THAT HE DID **NOT** POSSESS.

IN EARLY JULY 2002, CIA OFFICERS HELD SEVERAL MEETINGS AT CIA HEADQUARTERS TO DISCUSS THE POSSIBLE USE OF "NOVEL INTERROGATION METHODS" ON ABU ZUBAYDAH. THE LIST INCLUDED THE ATTENTION GRASP, WALLING, THE FACIAL HOLD . . .

. . . THE FACIAL SLAP, CRAMPED CONFINEMENT, WALLSTANDING, STRESS POSITIONS, WATERBOARDING, SLEEP DEPRIVATION, USE OF DIAPERS, USE OF INSECTS, AND MOCK BURIAL.

YES!

MAYBE?

DEPUTY ASSISTANT ATTORNEY GENERAL JOHN YOO TOLD THE CIA THAT THEIR INTERROGATION TECHNIQUE, HE BELIEVED, WOULD BE LAWFUL. HOWEVER, NATIONAL SECURITY ADVISOR CONDOLEEZZA RICE AND DEPUTY NATIONAL SECURITY ADVISOR JOHN HADLEY ASKED THE DEPARTMENT OF JUSTICE TO DELAY APPROVAL UNTIL THE CIA PROVIDED DETAILS ON THE PROGRAM AND WHY THEY ARE CONFIDENT IT WOULDN'T CAUSE LASTING HARM.

FINALLY, ON JULY 24, 2002, ATTORNEY GENERAL JOHN ASHCROFT VERBALLY APPROVED THE USE OF 10 INTERROGATION TECHNIQUES, REJECTING MOCK BURIAL AND WATERBOARDING. TWO DAYS LATER, HE APPROVED WATERBOARDING.

SEE? I TOLD YOU IT WOULD WORK!

THE INTERROGATION TEAM LATER DEEMED THE USE OF EITS A SUCCESS BECAUSE IT PROVIDED FURTHER EVIDENCE THAT ZUBAYDAH HAD *NOT* BEEN WITHHOLDING EVIDENCE.

CIA RECORDS INDICATE THAT THE FIRST CIA BRIEFING OF THE PRESIDENT ON THE PROGRAM OCCURRED ON APRIL 8, 2006. CIA RECORDS STATE THAT WHEN THE PRESIDENT WAS TOLD OF THE PROGRAM, HE EXPRESSED DISCOMFORT . . .

DETENTION OF ABU ZUBAYDAH AND THE DEVELOPMENT OF EITS

FROM AUGUST 4 TO 23, 2002, THE CIA SUBJECTED ABU ZUBAYDAH TO EITS, INCLUDING WATERBOARDING NEARLY 24 HOURS A DAY.

TWO CIA CONTRACTORS WERE THE ONLY PEOPLE TO HAVE PHYSICAL CONTACT WITH HIM. CIA MEDICAL PERSONNEL AND OTHER CIA "INTERROGATORS WITH WHOM HE IS FAMILIAR" WERE THERE ONLY TO OBSERVE. AFTER BEING IN ISOLATION FOR 47 DAYS, HE WAS BROUGHT IN.

SHACKLED AND HOODED, ZUBAYDAH WAS BROUGHT IN AND HIS TOWEL WAS REMOVED.

THE TOWEL WAS THEN PLACED AROUND HIS NECK AND HE WAS SLAMMED INTO THE CELL WALL.

A LARGE CONFINEMENT BOX MUCH LIKE A COFFIN WAS BROUGHT INTO THE ROOM.

THE INTERROGATORS THEN DEMANDED DETAILED INFORMATION ON TERRORIST ACTIVITIES.

EACH TIME ZUBAYDAH DENIED HAVING ANY INFORMATION HE WOULD RECEIVE A FACIAL SLAP OR FACIAL GRAB.

I DON'T KNOW

SLAP!

I DON'T KNOW

SLAP!

I DON'T KNOW

SLAP!

WHO ARE THE PEOPLE BEHIND THIS? GIVE ME THEIR NAMES! WHAT ARE THEIR PLANS?

AND THEN HE WOULD BE WATERBOARDED.

DETENTION AND INTERROGATION OF RIDHA AL-NAJJAR

THEN WE'LL CONTINUE WITH DISQUIETING SOUND TECHNIQUES, COLD TEMPERATURES, AND SLEEP DEPRIVATION.

RIDHA AL-NAJJAR WAS THE FIRST CIA DETAINEE TO BE HELD AT **DETENTION SITE COBALT**, CONSTRUCTED WITH CIA MONEY IN [REDACTED COUNTRY]. ARRESTED IN KARACHI IN A PAKISTANI RAID IN LATE MAY 2002, HE WAS IDENTIFIED AS A FORMER BODYGUARD OF USAMA BIN LADEN.

ON JULY 26, 2002, CIA OFFICERS, NONE OF WHOM WERE TRAINED IN THE USE OF EITS, PROPOSED PUTTING AL-NAJJAR IN ISOLATION AS THE FIRST STEP IN GAINING INFORMATION ON BIN LADEN AND HIS FAMILY.

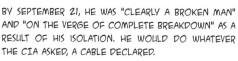

STARTING ON AUGUST 5, LOUD MUSIC SURROUNDED AL-NAJJAR'S ROOM, HE WAS FED TERRIBLE-TASTING FOOD, HE WAS KEPT FROM SLEEPING, AND HE WAS HOODED.

BY SEPTEMBER 21, HE WAS "CLEARLY A BROKEN MAN" AND "ON THE VERGE OF COMPLETE BREAKDOWN" AS A RESULT OF HIS ISOLATION. HE WOULD DO WHATEVER THE CIA ASKED, A CABLE DECLARED.

DETENTION AND DEATH OF GUL RAHMAN

IN NOVEMBER 2002, A NEW DETAINEE ARRIVED AT **DETENTION SITE COBALT** AND WAS DEEMED AN APPROPRIATE CANDIDATE FOR EITS. GUL RAHMAN, A SUSPECTED ISLAMIC EXTREMIST, WAS SHACKLED TO THE WALL OF HIS CELL IN A POSITION THAT REQUIRED HIM TO SIT ON THE BARE CONCRETE FLOOR WHILE WEARING ONLY A SWEATSHIRT. HIS OTHER CLOTHING HAD BEEN REMOVED WHEN HE HAD BEEN JUDGED UNCOOPERATIVE DURING AN EARLIER INTERROGATION.

GET OVER HERE NOW!

THE FOLLOWING MORNING, GUARDS FOUND GUL RAHMAN'S DEAD BODY. AN INTERNAL CIA REVIEW AND AUTOPSY FOUND THAT RAHMAN LIKELY DIED FROM HYPOTHERMIA--PROBABLY BECAUSE HE HAD TO SLEEP HALF-NAKED ON THE COLD CONCRETE FLOOR.

AT THE TIME, THE INITIAL CABLE TO CIA HEADQUARTERS INCLUDED A NUMBER OF MISSTATEMENTS AND OMISSIONS THAT WERE NOT DISCOVERED UNTIL A LATER INVESTIGATION INTO RAHMAN'S DEATH.

CONGRATULATIONS TO YOU! AND MAY YOUR GREAT WORK CONTINUE!

THE CIA OFFICER WHO HAD RECOMMENDED THE USE OF THE ENHANCED PROGRAM CAUSING RAHMAN'S DEATH RECEIVED NO PUNISHMENT. AND JUST FOUR MONTHS AFTER RAHMAN'S DEATH, IT WAS RECOMMENDED THAT THE OFFICER RECEIVE A CASH AWARD OF $2,500 FOR "CONSISTENTLY SUPERIOR WORK."

THE USE OF EITS WAS MORE WIDESPREAD THAN REPORTED IN CIA CABLES. THE COMMITTEE DISCOVERED UNREPORTED USAGE OF SLEEP DEPRIVATION WITH DETAINEE'S ARMS SHACKLED OVERHEAD, DIETARY MANIPULATION, EXPOSURE TO COLD TEMPERATURES, COLD SHOWERS, "ROUGH TAKEDOWNS," AND MOCK EXECUTIONS.

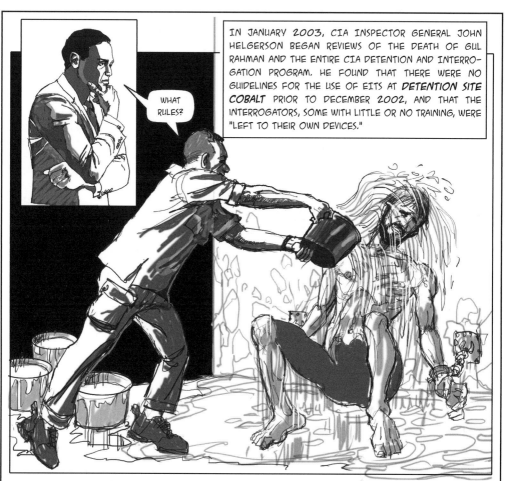

IN JANUARY 2003, CIA INSPECTOR GENERAL JOHN HELGERSON BEGAN REVIEWS OF THE DEATH OF GUL RAHMAN AND THE ENTIRE CIA DETENTION AND INTERROGATION PROGRAM. HE FOUND THAT THERE WERE NO GUIDELINES FOR THE USE OF EITS AT **DETENTION SITE COBALT** PRIOR TO DECEMBER 2002, AND THAT THE INTERROGATORS, SOME WITH LITTLE OR NO TRAINING, WERE "LEFT TO THEIR OWN DEVICES."

WHAT RULES?

IN LATE JANUARY 2003, CIA DIRECTOR GEORGE TENET SIGNED THE FIRST FORMAL INTERROGATION AND CONFINEMENT GUIDELINES FOR THE CIA PROGRAM. IN CONTRAST TO PROPOSALS FROM LATE 2001, WHICH REQUIRED THAT FACILITIES MEET U.S. PRISON STANDARDS, THESE WERE MINIMAL. DETENTION FACILITIES ONLY HAD TO MEET BASIC HEALTH NEEDS.

A FACILITY IN WHICH DETAINEES WERE SHACKLED IN COMPLETE DARKNESS AND ISOLATION WITH A BUCKET FOR HUMAN WASTE AND WITHOUT NOTABLE HEAT DURING THE WINTER WOULD MEET THE STANDARD.

CONSISTENT WITH INTERROGATION GUIDELINES, CIA OFFICERS COULD, AT THEIR DISCRETION, STRIP A DETAINEE NAKED, SHACKLE HIM IN THE STANDING POSITION FOR 72 HOURS, AND DOUSE HIM REPEATEDLY WITH COLD WATER WITHOUT APPROVAL FROM CIA HEADQUARTERS.

DETENTION AND INTERROGATION OF ABD AL-RAHIM AL-NASHIRI

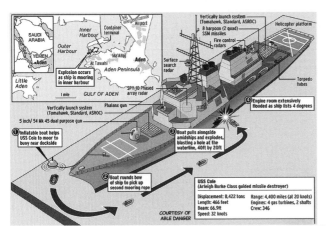

SAUDI ARABIA
YEMEN
•Aden
Inner Harbour
Container terminal
Outer Harbour
Airport
Ma'Allaj
Aden
At Tawahi
Aden Peninsula
Little Aden
GULF OF ADEN
1 mile

Explosion occurs as ship is mooring in inner harbour

Vertically launch system (Tomahawk, Standard, ASROC)
5 inch/ 54 Mk 45 dual purpose gun
Phalanx gun

Vertically launch system (Tomahawk, Standard, ASROC)
8 harpoon (2 quad) SSM missiles
Fire control radars
Helicopter platform

Surface search radar
SPY-1D Phased array radar

Torpedo tubes

Engine room extensively flooded as ship lists 4 degrees

① Inflatable boat helps USS Cole to moor to buoy near dockside

② Boat rounds bow of ship to pick up second mooring rope

③ Boat pulls alongside amidships and explodes, blasting a hole at the waterline, 40ft by 20ft

USS Cole
(Arleigh Burke Class guided missile destroyer)
Displacement: 8,422 tons
Length: 466 feet
Beam: 66.9ft
Speed: 32 knots
Range: 4,400 miles (at 20 knots)
Engines: 4 gas turbines, 2 shafts
Crew: 346

COURTESY OF ABLE DANGER

ABD AL-RAHIM AL-NASHIRI, ASSESSED BY THE CIA TO BE AN AL-QA'IDA "TERRORIST OPERATIONS PLANNER" "INTIMATELY INVOLVED" IN PLANNING THE USS COLE BOMBING AND THE 1998 EAST AFRICAN U.S. EMBASSY BOMBINGS, WAS CAPTURED IN THE UNITED ARAB EMIRATES IN OCTOBER 2002.

HE PROVIDED INFORMATION WHILE IN THE CUSTODY OF A FOREIGN GOVERNMENT, INCLUDING INFORMATION ON PLOTTING IN THE PERSIAN GULF, AND WAS THEN RENDERED TO THE CIA.

AT **DETENTION SITE GREEN**, AL-NASHIRI WAS INTERROGATED USING EITS, INCLUDING BEING SUBJECTED AT LEAST THREE TIMES TO WATERBOARDING.

HE WAS MOVED TO **DETENTION SITE BLUE** IN DECEMBER 2002. IN TOTAL, HE WAS SUBJECTED TO THE TECHNIQUES DURING AT LEAST FOUR SEPARATE PERIODS, AFTER WHICH HE WAS ASSESSED AS COMPLIANT AND COOPERATIVE.

I HEAR HE'S NEVER BEEN TRAINED OR CERTIFIED TO USE THE TECHNIQUE.

ON-SITE INTERROGATORS WANTED TO STOP USING THE EITS ON AL-NASHIRI, BUT A NEW CIA OFFICER ARRIVED ON THE SCENE. HE CAME WITH WORD THAT "THE AGENCY MANAGEMENT" BELIEVED THE INTERROGATORS HAD BEEN TOO LENIENT WITH AL-NASHIRI, AND THE TECHNIQUES SHOULD BE RESUMED.

HE PLACED AN AUTOMATIC PISTOL NEAR AL-NASHIRI'S HEAD

AND OPERATED A CORDLESS DRILL NEAR HIS BODY.

THE OFFICER, NOT TRAINED TO USE EITS, USED A SERIES OF UNAUTHORIZED INTERROGATION TECHNIQUES ON AL-NASHIRI. HE PLACED THE DETAINEE IN A "STANDING STRESS POSITION" WITH "HIS HANDS AFFIXED OVER HIS HEAD" FOR APPROXIMATELY TWO AND A HALF DAYS.

THE NEW CIA OFFICER ALSO EMPLOYED OTHER UNAUTHORIZED TECHNIQUES, SUCH AS GIVING ABD AL-RAHIM AL-NASHIRI A FORCED BATH USING A STIFF BRUSH, IMPLYING THAT HIS MOTHER WOULD BE BROUGHT BEFORE HIM AND SEXUALLY ABUSED, AND USING IMPROVISED STRESS POSITIONS THAT CAUSED CUTS AND BRUISES.

IN JANUARY 2003, A CIA CONTRACTOR ARRIVED TO CONDUCT PSYCHOLOGICAL TESTS ON AL-NASHIRI AND DECIDED HE WAS SUITABLE FOR THE "FULL RANGE" OF EITS. ONCE HIS "SENSE OF CONTROL" HAD BEEN ELIMINATED, THE USE OF EITS WOULD BE REDUCED.

LATER INTERVIEWED BY THE OFFICE OF INSPECTOR GENERAL, THE CHIEF OF **DETENTION SITE BLUE** SAID HE BELIEVED THE OFFICER WAS SENT FROM CIA HEADQUARTERS TO RESOLVE THE MATTER OF AL-NASHIRI'S COOPERATION AND BELIEVED THE OFFICER HAD PERMISSION TO USE THE TECHNIQUES. IN APRIL 2004, THE OFFICER WAS DISCIPLINED.

THE PROPOSED INTERROGATION PLAN CAUSED THE CIA CHIEF OF INTERROGATIONS TO RETIRE AND "NO LONGER BE ASSOCIATED" WITH THE PROGRAM. HE PROCLAIMED THE PROGRAM "A TRAIN WRECK WAITING TO HAPPEN."

I THANK YOU, ALLAH!

U.S DETENTION

BEGINNING IN JUNE 2003, AL-NASHIRI WAS TRANSFERRED TO FIVE DIFFERENT CIA DETENTION FACILITIES BEFORE BEING MOVED TO U.S. MILITARY CUSTODY ON SEPTEMBER 5, 2006. OVER THE YEARS, HE ACCUSED THE CIA STAFF OF DRUGGING OR POISONING HIS FOOD AND COMPLAINED OF BODY PAIN AND INSOMNIA.

EVERY ONE OF THESE IS A DEBRIEFING OF AL-NASHIRI, AND NONE OF THEM ARE WORTH A FOLLOW-UP!

IN OCTOBER 2004, 21 MONTHS AFTER THE FINAL DOCUMENTED USE OF EITS AGAINST AL-NASHIRI, THE CIA DISSEMINATED 145 REPORTS ON HIS DEBRIEFINGS, BUT THERE WAS "ESSENTIALLY NO ACTIONABLE INFORMATION," AS ONE INTERROGATOR CONCLUDED.

HE PROVIDED INFORMATION ON PAST OPERATIONAL PLOTTING, ASSOCIATES HE EXPECTED TO PARTICIPATE IN PLOTS, DETAILS ON COMPLETED OPERATIONS, AND BACKGROUND MATERIAL ON AL-QA'IDA, BUT NOTHING THAT COULD BE USED TO THWART FUTURE ATTACKS.

DETENTION AND INTERROGATION OF RAMZI BIN AL-SHIBH

AS EARLY AS SEPTEMBER 15, 2001, RAMZI BIN AL-SHIBH WAS ASSESSED BY THE CIA TO BE A FACILITATOR OF THE 9/11 ATTACKS AND AN ASSOCIATE OF THE HIJACKERS. WHILE TARGETING ANOTHER TERRORIST, PAKISTANI OFFICIALS UNEXPECTEDLY CAPTURED HIM ON SEPTEMBER 11, 2002. APPROXIMATELY FIVE MONTHS LATER, IN FEBRUARY 2003, BIN AL-SHIBH WAS RENDERED INTO CIA CUSTODY.

THEY SAY THAT FOOD TASTES BETTER THIS WAY!

AFTER BIN AL-SHIBH WAS INTERROGATED USING EITS FOR AN ESTIMATED 34 DAYS, THE CIA CONCLUDED THAT HE WAS NOT A SENIOR MEMBER OF AL-QA'IDA AND NOT IN A POSITION TO KNOW DETAILS OF THEIR PLANS.

HOWEVER, CIA HEADQUARTERS BELIEVED MORE INFORMATION COULD STILL BE GAINED FROM THE DETAINEE AND ORDERED HIM TRANSFERRED TO **DETENTION SITE BLUE.**

AFTER MEDICAL AND PHYSICAL ASSESSMENTS, THE SO-CALLED "SENSORY DISLOCATION" PHASE NOW PROPOSED FOR USE ON BIN AL-SHIBH INCLUDED SHAVING HIS HEAD AND FACE, EXPOSING HIM TO A LOUD NOISE IN A WHITE ROOM WITH WHITE LIGHTS, "KEEPING HIM UNCLOTHED AND SUBJECTED TO UNCOMFORTABLE COOL TEMPERATURES," AND SHACKLING HIM "HAND AND FOOT WITH ARMS OUTSTRETCHED" OVERHEAD.

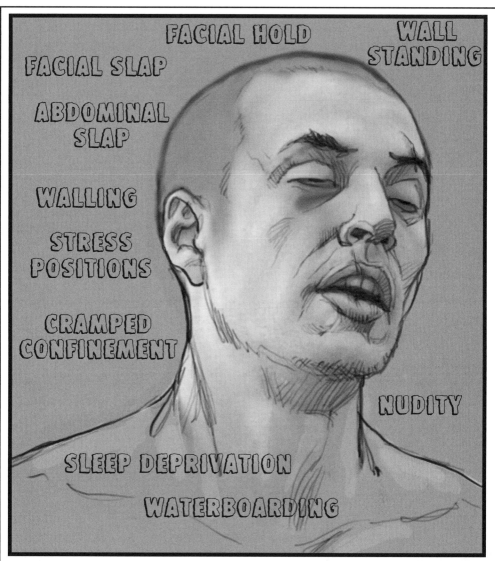

THE INTERROGATION PHASE INCLUDED NEAR-CONSTANT INTERROGATIONS, CONTINUED SENSORY DEPRIVATION, A LIQUID DIET, AND SLEEP DEPRIVATION. IN ADDITION, EITS WOULD BE USED, INCLUDING "ATTENTION GRASP, WALLING, THE FACIAL HOLD, THE FACIAL SLAP, . . . THE ABDOMINAL SLAP, CRAMPED CONFINEMENT, WALL STANDING, STRESS POSITIONS, SLEEP DEPRIVATION BEYOND 72 HOURS, AND THE WATER BOARD AS APPROPRIATE TO [RAMZI BIN AL-SHIBH'S] LEVEL OF RESISTANCE."

BASED ON VERSIONS OF THIS INTERROGATION PLAN, AT LEAST SIX OTHER DETAINEES WERE STRIPPED AND SHACKLED NUDE, PLACED IN THE STANDING POSITION FOR SLEEP DEPRIVATION, OR SUBJECTED TO OTHER TECHNIQUES PRIOR TO BEING QUESTIONED.

FIVE OF THESE DETAINEES WERE SHACKLED NAKED IN THE STANDING POSITION WITH THEIR HANDS ABOVE THEIR HEADS IMMEDIATELY AFTER THEIR MEDICAL CHECK.

WHEN CIA INTERROGATORS ASSESSED THAT BIN AL-SHIBH WAS COOPERATIVE AND DID NOT HAVE ANY ADDITIONAL KNOWLEDGE TO OFFER, CIA HEADQUARTERS DISAGREED. THEY ORDERED INTERROGATORS TO CONTINUE USING EITS. AS A RESULT, CIA OFFICERS CONTINUED TO USE EITS ON BIN AL-SHIBH FOR APPROXIMATELY THREE MORE WEEKS. STILL, BIN AL-SHIBH DID NOT PROVIDE THE INFORMATION THEY SOUGHT.

DID YOU HEAR WHAT BIN AL-SHIBH JUST TOLD US?

OF COURSE! HE SAID THE SAME THING THREE YEARS AGO!

CIA RECORDS INDICATE THAT RAMZI BIN AL-SHIBH'S INTER-ROGATORS WERE UNAWARE OF THE INTELLIGENCE HE HAD PROVIDED WHILE IN FOREIGN GOVERNMENT CUSTODY. ON MANY OCCASIONS, INTERROGATORS BELIEVED THEY HAD PRODUCED NEW INFORMATION WHEN HE WAS MERELY REPEATING WHAT HE HAD SHARED BEFORE.

BIN AL-SHIBH WAS SUBJECTED TO INTERROGATION TECH-NIQUES AND CONFINEMENT CONDITIONS THAT WERE NOT APPROVED BY CIA HEADQUARTERS, SUCH AS WHEN HE FAILED TO SAY "SIR" OR ANSWERED WITH A "BLANK STARE" OR COM-PLAINED OF STOMACH PAIN.

PLEASE, PLEASE, SIRS! A LITTLE LIGHT, PLEASE ...

HE WAS KEPT IN TOTAL DARKNESS TO HEIGHTEN HIS SENSE OF FEAR ... DESPITE CIA POLICY TO KEEP DETAINEES UNDER CONSTANT LIGHT.

THERE, THERE, SIR. CAN YOU NOT SEE HIM NOW?

NO, I DON'T! THERE'S NO ONE THERE.

AND N-N-NOW WHERE AM I G-G-GOING?

CIA PSYCHOLOGICAL ASSESSMENTS OF BIN AL-SHIBH WERE SLOW TO RECOGNIZE THE ONSET OF PSYCHOLOGICAL PROBLEMS CAUSED BY HIS LONG-TERM ISOLATION AND FEAR OF A RETURN TO USING EITS. HIS SYMPTOMS INCLUDED VISIONS, PARANOIA, INSOMNIA, AND ATTEMPTS AT SELF-HARM.

IN APRIL 2005, A CIA PSYCHOLOGIST STATED THAT BIN AL-SHIBH "HAS REMAINED IN SOCIAL ISOLATION" FOR AS LONG AS TWO AND A HALF YEARS, AND IT WAS HAVING A "CLEAR AND ESCALATING EFFECT ON HIS PSYCHOLOGICAL FUNCTIONING."

THE PSYCHOLOGIST POINTED OUT THAT HE HAD BEEN A "HIGH- FUNCTIONING INDIVIDUAL, MAKING HIS DETERIORA-TION ... MORE ALARMING." THE ASSESSMENT HELPED BRING ABOUT HIS TRANSFERAL TO U.S. MILITARY CUSTODY AT GUAN-TANAMO BAY ON SEPTEMBER 5, 2006, WHERE HE WAS PLACED ON ANTIPSYCHOTIC MEDICATION.

THE CIA DISSEMINATED 109 INTELLIGENCE REPORTS FROM INTERROGATIONS OF RAMZI BIN AL-SHIBH, CONCLUDING THAT MANY OF HIS STATEMENTS "HAVE BEEN SPECULATIVE, AND MANY OF THE DETAILS COULD BE FOUND IN MEDIA ACCOUNTS" APPEARING BEFORE HIS DETAINMENT.

THEY CONCLUDED THAT "THE OVERALL QUALITY OF HIS REPORTING HAS STEADILY DECLINED SINCE 2003."

WE SHOULD HAVE GOTTEN TO HIM BEFORE THESE HELLISH TWO YEARS!

HE'S ALL YOURS, GENTLEMEN!

DETENTION AND INTERROGATION OF KHALID SHAYK MOHAMMAD

IN THE SPRING OF 2001, KHALID SHAYKH MOHAMMAD (KSM) WAS CAPTURED THANKS TO A SINGLE CIA SOURCE. THE INTELLIGENCE LED THE CIA AND PAKISTANI AUTHORITIES DIRECTLY TO KSM, WHO WAS HELD IN PAKISTANI CUSTODY FOR A MONTH.

WHILE IN PAKISTANI CUSTODY, KSM WAS SUBJECTED TO SOME SLEEP DEPRIVATION, BUT THERE WERE NO INDICATIONS OF OTHER COERCIVE TECHNIQUES. HE DENIED KNOWLEDGE OF ANY ATTACK PLANS, WHERE USAMA BIN LADEN OR AYMAN AL-ZAWAHIRI MIGHT BE, BUT HE DID PROVIDE LIMITED INFORMATION ON VARIOUS AL-QA'IDA LEADERS AND OPERATIVES WHO HAD ALREADY BEEN CAPTURED.

IT WAS SUCCESSFULLY ARGUED THAT CIA CONTRACTORS SHOULD TAKE OVER HIS INTERROGATION UPON HIS ARRIVAL AT **DETENTION SITE BLUE.** ON MARCH 3, 2003, CIA HEADQUARTERS APPROVED AN INTERROGATION PLAN THAT SPECIFIED KSM "BE SUBJECTED TO IMMEDIATE INTERROGATION TECHNIQUES . . . [THAT] WILL INCREASE IN INTENSITY FROM STANDARD TO ENHANCED . . . COMMENSURATE WITH HIS LEVEL OF RESISTANCE UNTIL HE INDICATES INITIAL COOPERATION."

I KNOW OF NO ATTACK PLANS, NOR HAVE ANY IDEA OF WHERE BIN LADEN OR AL-ZAWAHIRI MIGHT BE.

HE IS A BAD ONE.

FROM KSM'S ARRIVAL AT **DETENTION SITE BLUE** UNTIL MARCH 9, 2003, CIA CONTRACTORS USED EITS AGAINST HIM THAT INCLUDED: NUDITY, STANDING SLEEP DEPRIVATION, THE ATTENTION GRAB, THE INSULT SLAP, THE FACIAL GRAB, THE ABDOMINAL SLAP, THE KNEELING STRESS POSITION, AND WALLING. KSM WAS ALSO SUBJECTED TO WATERBOARDING.

WHEN THESE METHODS SEEMED TO MAKE THE DETAINEE "CLAM UP," IT WAS DECIDED TO TRY A SOFTER APPROACH. ON MARCH 9, CALLED "THE BEST SESSION HELD TO DATE" BY THE CIA INTERROGATION TEAM, KSM FABRICATED INFORMATION INDICATING THAT JAFFAR AL-TAYYAR AND JOSÉ PADILLA WERE PLOTTING TOGETHER. THIS FABRICATION RESULTED IN THE CAPTURE AND DETENTION OF TWO INNOCENT INDIVIDUALS.

PLEASE, PLEASE . . . ENOUGH! I'LL DO WHATEVER YOU WANT ME TO DO!

IT TOOK A LOT, BUT WE'VE GOT HIM!

WATERBOARDING

WATER IS POURED OVER A CLOTH COVERING THE BREATHING PASSAGES OF THE FACE, CAUSING THE DETAINEE TO EXPERIENCE THE SENSATION OF DROWNING.

GROWTH OF THE CIA'S DETENTION AND INTERROGATION PROGRAM

I WANT TO KNOW WHAT HE KNOWS, AND I WANT TO KNOW IT FAST!

IN MARCH 2003, **DETENTION SITE BLUE** REPORTEDLY RECEIVED A PHONE CALL FROM CIA HEADQUARTERS CONVEYING THE VIEWS OF DIRECTOR OF OPERATIONS JAMES PAVITT ON KSM'S INTERROGATION.

THE SITE'S MEDICAL OFFICER LATER WROTE IN AN E-MAIL THAT CIA INTERROGATORS "FELT THAT THE [WATERBOARD] WAS THE BIG STICK AND THAT HQ WAS MORE OR LESS DEMANDING THAT IT BE USED EARLY AND OFTEN."

ON MARCH 10, 2003, KSM WAS SUBJECTED TO THE FIRST OF 15 SEPARATE WATERBOARDING SESSIONS. THIS ONE LASTED 30 MINUTES, 10 MORE THAN ANTICIPATED.

STOP, STOP!!

THIS WAS IMMEDIATELY FOLLOWED BY THE USE OF A HORIZONTAL STRESS POSITION THAT HAD NOT BEEN PREVIOUSLY APPROVED BY CIA HEADQUARTERS.

THE CHIEF OF BASE, WORRIED ABOUT THE LEGAL IMPLICATIONS, PROHIBITED THE ON-SITE MEDICAL OFFICER FROM REPORTING ON THE INTERROGATION DIRECTLY TO THE OFFICE OF MEDICAL SERVICES OUTSIDE OF OFFICIAL CIA CABLE TRAFFIC.

THAT IS WHAT YOU WANT TO HIT!

TWO DAYS LATER, KSM PROVIDED INFORMATION ON PLOTS TARGETING HEATHROW AIRPORT AND CANARY WHARF. HE CLAIMED THAT HE HAD SHOWN A SKETCH OF A BUILDING IN CANARY WHARF TO AMMAR AL-BALUCHI, A TERRORIST THEN STILL AT LARGE AND KSM'S NEPHEW.

CIA INTERROGATORS DEEMED THAT KSM'S TALK ABOUT LONDON WAS AN EFFORT TO AVOID DISCUSSING PLOTS INSIDE THE UNITED STATES. THEY RESPONDED BY WATERBOARDING HIM TWICE THAT DAY.

CIA RECORDS STATE THAT KSM'S "ABDOMEN WAS SOMEWHAT DISTENDED AND HE EXPRESSED WATER WHEN THE ABDOMEN WAS PRESSED." HE WAS ALSO SUBJECTED TO THE ATTENTION GRASP, INSULT SLAP, ABDOMINAL SLAP, AND WALLING THAT DAY.

ON MARCH 13, 2003, AFTER KSM AGAIN DENIED THAT AL-QA'IDA WAS PLANNING OPERATIONS INSIDE THE UNITED STATES, INTERROGATORS BEGAN A "DAY OF INTENSIVE WATERBOARD SESSIONS." DURING THE FIRST OF THREE PLANNED SESSIONS, INTERROGATORS HELD KSM'S LIPS AND DIRECTED THE WATER TO HIS MOUTH.

DURING ANOTHER SESSION, THEY WAITED FOR KSM TO TALK BEFORE POURING WATER OVER HIS MOUTH.

ON MARCH 18, 2003, PERSONNEL NOTED THAT "KSM WILL SELECTIVELY LIE, PROVIDE PARTIAL TRUTHS, AND MISDIRECT WHEN HE BELIEVES HE WILL NOT BE FOUND OUT AND HELD ACCOUNTABLE."

NO, NO, STOP! YOU PEOPLE MADE ME WANT TO LIE ABOUT AL-TAYYAR!

AFTER FIVE WATERBOARDING SESSIONS IN 25 HOURS, CIA HEADQUARTERS REEVALUATED THE USE OF THE METHOD IN KSM'S CASE. BUT DESPITE FEELINGS THAT IT COULD "POISON THE WELL," USE OF THE TECHNIQUE WAS CONTINUED ANOTHER 10 DAYS. DURING ONE OF THOSE SESSIONS, INTERROGATORS USED THEIR HANDS TO MAINTAIN A ONE-INCH-DEEP "POOL" OF WATER OVER HIS NOSE AND MOUTH . . .

PLEASE DON'T TELL THEM WHERE THIS CAME FROM, BUT I SWEAR THAT JAFFAR AL-TAYYAR TOOK PART IN THE HEATHROW AIRPORT PLOT!

KSM APPEARED "MORE INCLINED TO MAKE ACCURATE DISCLOSURES WHEN HE BELIEVES PEOPLE, E-MAILS, OR OTHER SOURCE MATERIAL" WERE AVAILABLE TO CHECK HIS RESPONSES.

DUE TO KSM'S INCONSISTENT INFORMATION CONCERNING AL-TAYYAR, THE INTERROGATORS CHOSE TO WATERBOARD HIM AGAIN ON MARCH 19. BUT THEY INSTRUCTED HIM TO SPEAK ONLY IF AND WHEN HE WAS REVEALING INFORMATION ON THE "NEXT ATTACK ON AMERICA." THE TORTURE CONTINUED WITH ATTENTION GRABS, INSULT SLAPS, WALLING, WATER DOUSING, AND, YES, WATERBOARDING.

MY SONS? WHY ARE THEY HANGING PHOTOS OF MY SONS?

ON MARCH 20, 2003, KSM CONTINUED TO BE SUBJECTED TO EITS, INCLUDING A PERIOD OF "INTENSE QUESTIONING AND WALLING."

FINALLY, THE DETENTION SITE PERSONNEL HUNG A PICTURE OF HIS SONS IN HIS CELL AS A WAY TO "[HEIGHTEN] HIS IMAGINATION" CONCERNING WHERE THEY WERE, WHO HAD THEM, AND WHAT WAS IN STORE FOR THEM.

APPARENTLY THIS DIDN'T CAUSE ANY CHANGE IN KSM'S BEHAVIOR, AND WATERBOARDING WAS AGAIN USED OVER THE NEXT TWO DAYS IN AN ATTEMPT TO DISCOVER WHETHER KSM HAD INTENDED TO USE "TWO TO THREE UNKNOWN BLACK AMERICAN MUSLIM CONVERTS WHO WERE CURRENTLY IN AFGHANISTAN [TO] . . . CONDUCT ATTACKS" ON GAS STATIONS IN THE UNITED STATES.

KSM "FLATLY DENIED" THAT HE HAD MADE ANY EFFORTS TO RECRUIT AFRICAN AMERICAN MUSLIM CONVERTS BEFORE BEING WATERBOARDED. THREATENED WITH A SECOND WATER-BOARDING, HE ADMITTED THAT PERHAPS HE HAD TOLD MAJID KHAN THAT HE SHOULD SEE IF HE COULD MAKE CONTACT WITH MEMBERS OF THE BLACK AMERICAN MUSLIM CONVERT COMMUNITY.

ON MARCH 24, 2003, KSM UNDERWENT HIS FIFTEENTH AND FINAL WATERBOARDING SESSION DUE TO HIS "INTRANSIGENCE" IN FAILING TO IDENTIFY SUSPECTED ABU BAKR AL-AZDI OPERATIONS IN THE UNITED STATES AND FOR HAVING "LIED ABOUT POISON AND BIOLOGICAL WAR-FARE PROGRAMS."

WITH THE EXCEPTION OF SLEEP DEPRIVATION, WHICH CONTINUED FOR ONE MORE DAY, THE USE OF EITS AGAINST KSM ENDED ABRUPTLY ON MARCH 24, 2003. THERE ARE NO CIA RECORDS DIRECTING THE INTERROGATION TEAM TO CEASE NOR ANY DOCUMENTATION EXPLAINING THE DECISION.

ON APRIL 3, 2003, THE INTERAGENCY INTELLIGENCE COMMITTEE ON TERRORISM PRODUCED AN ASSESSMENT OF KSM'S INTELLIGENCE ENTITLED "PRECIOUS TRUTHS, SURROUNDED BY A BODYGUARD OF LIES." THEY CONCLUDED THAT KSM WAS WITHHOLDING OR LYING ABOUT TERRORIST PLOTS AND OPERATIVES TARGETING THE UNITED STATES.

WELL, THEY FINALLY GOT IT RIGHT!

IT CAN'T BE LONG, SIR. I WOULDN'T WORRY.

ON APRIL 24, 2003, FBI DIRECTOR ROBERT MUELLER SOUGHT FBI ACCESS TO KSM TO BETTER UNDERSTAND CIA REPORTING ABOUT ENEMY THREATS TO U.S. CITIES. THE CIA REPLIED THAT THE FBI COULD NOT BE PROVIDED ACCESS UNTIL KSM WAS TRANSFERRED TO GUANTANAMO BAY, WHICH DID NOT OCCUR UNTIL SEPTEMBER 2006.

I KNOW I CAN HELP YOU, SIR! I KNOW EXACTLY WHO IS BEHIND THIS!

IN AN E-MAIL CONCERNING KSM, A CIA OFFICER NOTED THAT "WHAT KSM'S DOING IS FAIRLY TYPICAL OF OTHER DETAINEES . . . KSM, KHALLAD [BIN ATTASH], AND OTHERS ARE DOING WHAT MAKES SENSE IN THEIR SITUATION--PRETEND COOPERATION." AFTER KSM WAS TRANSFERRED TO **DETENTION SITE BLACK**, PERSONNEL AT A FORMER HOLDING SITE WROTE THAT HE "MAY NEVER BE FULLY FORTHCOMING AND HONEST" ON THE TOPIC OF USAMA BIN LADEN'S WHEREABOUTS.

DESPITE REPEATED CHALLENGES, KSM MAINTAINED THAT HE DIDN'T KNOW BIN LADEN'S LOCATION.

THESE ARE ALL THE REPORTS YOU HAVE FILED?

YES, AND THESE ARE THE ONES THAT HAVE BEEN FABRICATED.

THE CIA DISSEMINATED 831 INTELLIGENCE REPORTS FROM INFORMATION PROVIDED BY KSM OVER THREE AND A HALF YEARS. AMOUNTING TO NEARLY 15% OF ALL DETAINEE REPORTING, MORE THAN ANY OTHER DETAINEE PROVIDED, A SIGNIFICANT AMOUNT OF KSM'S INTELLIGENCE REPORTS WERE LATER IDENTIFIED AS FABRICATED.

2003 WAS THE MOST ACTIVE PERIOD OF THE CIA'S DETENTION AND INTERROGATION PROGRAM. OF THE 119 DETAINEES IDENTIFIED BY THE SSCI AS HELD BY THE CIA, 53 (44.5%) WERE BROUGHT INTO CUSTODY DURING THAT YEAR. OF THE 39 DETAINEES SUBJECTED TO EITS, 17 (44.1%) WERE SUBJECTED TO THEM BETWEEN JANUARY AND AUGUST 2003.

IN MAY 2004, THE SAME AMBASSADOR SOUGHT DOCUMENTS AUTHORIZING ABU GHRAIB'S DETAINMENT PROGRAM AFTER ABUSES IN THE MILITARY PRISON IN IRAQ CAME TO LIGHT.

DEPUTY SECRETARY OF STATE RICHARD ARMITAGE ONCE AGAIN QUESTIONED THE EFFICACY OF THE PROGRAM AND THE VALUE OF INTELLIGENCE IT HAD PRODUCED.

AT LEAST 17 CIA DETAINEES WERE SUBJECTED TO EITS WITHOUT CIA HEADQUARTERS' AUTHORIZATION AT A FACILITY THAT WAS NOT DESIGNATED. CIA HEADQUARTERS FAILED TO RESPOND TO, INQUIRE ABOUT, OR INVESTIGATE THE ISSUE.

IN AUGUST 2003, THE U.S. AMBASSADOR OF [REDACTED COUNTRY] CONTACTED THE STATE DEPARTMENT OFFICIALS TO ENSURE THEY WERE AWARE OF THE DETAINMENT FACILITY LOCATED IN THE COUNTRY. HE WAS TOLD...

NO... NO ONE IN THE DEPARTMENT, INCLUDING THE SECRETARY OF STATE, HAS BEEN INFORMED OF THIS SITUATION!

YOU CUT US OUT OF THE PROCESS AND NOW WANT US TO SUPPORT IT?

WE QUESTION THE ENTIRE THING!

OVER THE COURSE OF THE PROGRAM, NUMEROUS DETAINEES WERE SUBJECTED TO THE TECHNIQUES BY **UNTRAINED INTERROGATORS.** THE CIA DID NOT BEGIN ITS TRAINING COURSE UNTIL NOVEMBER 2002, AT WHICH TIME NINE DETAINEES HAD BEEN SUBJECTED TO EITS.

AFTER JANUARY 28, 2003, GUIDELINES ONLY REQUIRED INTERROGATORS BE "APPROPRIATELY SCREENED," REVIEW THE GUIDELINES, AND RECEIVE "APPROPRIATE TRAINING" IN IMPLEMENTATION OF THESE GUIDELINES.

NOW WHAT THE HECK AM I SUPPOSED TO DO?

STOP! PLEASE STOP... THAT IS SO COLD!

ARSALA KHAN, AN AFGHAN NATIONAL IN HIS MID-50S WRONGLY ACCUSED OF ASSISTING USAMA BIN LADEN, WAS DETAINED FOR A MONTH AND SUBJECTED TO 56 HOURS OF SLEEP DEPRIVATION. IT WAS DETERMINED THAT HE HAD BEEN WRONGLY ACCUSED, AND IT WAS RECOMMENDED THAT HE RECEIVE A CASH PAYMENT. BUT HE WAS NOT RELEASED UNTIL FOUR YEARS LATER!

I NEED SLEEP, I TELL YOU, I SWEAR I'M INNOCENT!

CIA HEADQUARTERS APPROVED REQUESTS TO USE WATER DOUSING, NUDITY, THE ABDOMINAL SLAP, AND DIETARY MANIPULATION DESPITE THE FACT THAT THE DEPARTMENT OF JUSTICE HAD NOT YET APPROVED THEIR USE.

IN THE FALL OF 2003, CIA OFFICERS IN [REDACTED COUNTRY] EXAMINED THE RECORDS OF 44 DETAINEES, ALL IN SOLITARY CONFINEMENT, WHO HAD BEEN HELD FOR MONTHS AND SOMETIMES MORE THAN A YEAR, AND DECIDED THAT THERE WAS NOT ENOUGH EVIDENCE TO HOLD MOST OF THEM. THE VAST MAJORITY WERE THEN RELEASED, WITH SOME RECEIVING CIA PAYMENTS FOR HAVING BEEN HELD IN DETENTION.

THOUGH CIA HEADQUARTERS INFORMED THE DEPARTMENT OF JUSTICE IN JULY 2002 "THAT STEPS WILL BE TAKEN TO ENSURE THAT [ABU ZUBAYDAH'S] INJURY IS NOT . . . EXACERBATED BY THE USE OF THESE [ENHANCED INTERROGATION] METHODS," THEY INFORMED INTERROGATORS THAT INTERROGATION WOULD TAKE "PRECEDENCE" OVER HIS MEDICAL CARE.

HE WAS KEPT NAKED, FED A "BARE BONES" LIQUID DIET, AND SUBJECTED TO NONSTOP USE OF EITS. ON AUGUST 15, 2002, MEDICAL PERSONNEL REPORTED THE "STEADY DETE-RIORATION" OF HIS SURGICAL WOUND. LATER ONE OF HIS EYES BEGAN TO DETERIORATE.

BUT I AM SICK. YOUR OWN DOCTOR TOLD ME SO!

IN APRIL 2003, ABU HAZIM AND ABD AL-KARIM EACH BROKE A FOOT TRYING TO ESCAPE CAPTURE AND WERE PLACED IN CASTS.

CIA CABLES STATED THAT INTERROGATORS SHOULD "FOREGO CRAMPED CONFINEMENT, STRESS POSITIONS, WALLING, AND VERTICAL SHACKLING (DUE TO THEIR INJURY)." BOTH WERE SUBJECTED TO ONE OR MORE EITS.

WHY . . . WHY AM I HERE?!

SMASH!

STOP!

YOU'RE GOING TO KILL YOURSELF!

EXACTLY WHAT I WANT TO DO!

LATE IN HIS DETENTION, ABD AL-RAHIM AL-NASHIRI ENGAGED IN REPEATED BELLIGERENT ACTS, INCLUDING THROWING FOOD TRAYS, ATTEMPTS TO ASSAULT PERSONNEL, AND ATTEMPTS TO DAMAGE ITEMS IN HIS CELL-- ALL BECAUSE OF THE AUSTERE CONDITIONS OF HIS CONFINEMENT.

MAJID KHAN ENGAGED IN ACTS OF SELF-HARM THAT INCLUDED ATTEMPTS TO CUT HIS WRIST ON TWO OCCASIONS, AN ATTEMPT TO CHEW INTO HIS ARM AT THE INNER ELBOW, AN ATTEMPT TO CUT A VEIN AT THE TOP OF HIS FOOT, AND AN ATTEMPT TO CUT INTO HIS SKIN AT THE ELBOW JOINT USING A FILED TOOTHBRUSH.

SEVERAL TIMES IN EARLY 2003, CIA GENERAL COUNSEL SCOTT MULLER EXPRESSED CONCERN THAT THE CIA'S PROGRAM MIGHT BE INCONSISTENT WITH THE ADMINISTRATION'S CLAIM THAT ITS TREATMENT OF DETAINEES WAS HUMANE. THE WHITE HOUSE PRESS SECRETARY WAS ADVISED . . .

SIMPLY DO NOT USE THE TERM HUMANE TREATMENT WHEN TALKING ABOUT THE DETENTION OF AL-QA'IDA AND TALIBAN PERSONNEL!

THERE ALSO WERE DISCUSSIONS AS TO WHETHER THE CIA'S TREATMENT WAS CONSISTENT WITH THE FIFTH, EIGHTH, AND FOURTEENTH AMENDMENTS.

IN JULY 2003, WHILE THE CIA SOUGHT REAFFIRMATION FROM THE NATIONAL SECURITY ADVISOR ON THE USE OF EITS, THE CIA STOPPED APPROVING THEIR USE AND INSTEAD APPROVED "STANDARD" INTERROGATION TECHNIQUES, NOT CONSIDERED AS COERCIVE AS EITS.

NOW REMEMBER, HE GETS ONLY 70 HOURS OF SLEEP DEPRIVATION!

WE WARN YOU THAT THE TERMINATION OF THIS PROGRAM WILL RESULT IN LOSS OF LIFE, POSSIBLY EXTENSIVELY!

ON JULY 29, 2003, IN A PRESENTATION TO SELECT GOVERNMENT OFFICIALS, INCLUDING VICE PRESIDENT DICK CHENEY, NATIONAL SECURITY ADVISOR CONDOLEEZZA RICE, AND ATTORNEY GENERAL JOHN ASHCROFT, THE CIA PROVIDED AN OVERVIEW OF THE DETENTION AND INTERROGATION PROGRAM WITH MANY INACCURATE REPRESENTATIONS. CHENEY CONCLUDED, AND RICE AGREED, "THAT THE CIA WAS EXECUTING ADMINISTRATION POLICY IN CARRYING OUT ITS INTERROGATION PROGRAM."

THE NATIONAL SECURITY COUNCIL (NSC) PRINCIPALS PRESENT AT THE JULY 2003 MEETING CONCLUDED THAT IT WAS NOT NECESSARY TO BRIEF THE FULL COMMITTEE. IN JUSTIFICATION, A CIA E-MAIL NOTED THAT THIS WAS TO AVOID PRESS DISCLOSURES AND ADDED, "[SECRETARY OF STATE] POWELL WOULD BLOW HIS STACK IF HE WERE TO BE BRIEFED ON WHAT'S BEEN GOING ON."

YES, HE'S HEARD ALL YOUR ARGUMENTS, BUT THE DEPARTMENT IS TIRED OF "TAKING HITS" FOR YOUR "GHOST DETAINEES."

PRIOR TO A NATIONAL SECURITY COUNCIL MEETING ON SEPTEMBER 14, 2004, DEPUTY SECRETARY OF DEFENSE PAUL WOLFOWITZ INFORMED THE CIA THAT HE WOULD NOT SUPPORT THEIR POSITION THAT NOTIFYING THE INTERNATIONAL COMMITTEE OF THE RED CROSS (ICRC) OF ALL DETAINEES IN U.S. CUSTODY WOULD HARM U.S. NATIONAL SECURITY.

YOU DON'T EXPECT ME TO BELIEVE YOU WERE TAUGHT NOTHING ABOUT THIS!

N-NOTHING.

THE CIA'S OFFICE OF THE INSPECTOR GENERAL (OIG) WAS FIRST INFORMED OF THE DETENTION AND INTERRO-GATION PROGRAM IN NOVEMBER 2002, NINE MONTHS AFTER ABU ZUBAYDAH BECAME THEIR FIRST DETAINEE. NUMEROUS CIA OFFICERS EXPRESSED CONCERN ABOUT THEIR LACK OF PREPAREDNESS FOR CARRYING OUT THE EITS. OTHERS SHOWED CONCERN FOR THEIR LACK OF LINGUISTIC AND CULTURAL KNOWLEDGE; YET OTHERS QUESTIONED FAULTY ASSUMPTIONS ABOUT WHAT THE CIA BELIEVED DETAINEES WOULD KNOW.

IN ITS REVIEW OF THE DETENTION AND INTERROGATION PROGRAM IN JANUARY 2004, THE OIG DETAILED DIFFERENCES BETWEEN DESCRIBED TECHNIQUES AND APPLIED ONES, THE USE OF UNAU-THORIZED ONES, AND PROBLEMS IN OVERSIGHT.

WITHOUT THE USE OF SUCH TECHNIQUES, WE AND OUR ALLIES WOULD HAVE SUFFERED MAJOR TERRORIST ATTACKS INVOLVING HUNDREDS IF NOT THOUSANDS OF CASUALTIES.

DEPUTY DIRECTOR FOR OPERATIONS JAMES PAVITT IN A SPECIAL REVIEW CONCLUDED THAT "OUR EFFORTS HAVE THWARTED ATTACKS AND SAVED LIVES."

A REVIEW OF CIA RECORDS FOUND THAT THESE REPRESENTATIONS WERE ALMOST ENTIRELY INACCURATE.

THOUGH AN ASSESSMENT OF THE EFFECTIVENESS OF THE INTERROGATION PROGRAM BY THE CIA IN MID-2004 CALLED THE PROGRAM "A SUCCESS," IT CONCLUDED THAT DETENTION AND INTERROGATION ACTIVITIES SHOULD *NOT* BE CONDUCTED BY THE CIA BUT BY "EXPERIENCED U.S. LAW ENFORCEMENT OFFICERS" AND THE CIA "SHOULD FOCUS ON ITS CORE MISSION: CLANDESTINE INTELLIGENCE ACTIVITIES."

IN JANUARY 2004, GERMAN CITIZEN KHALID AL-MASRI WAS DETAINED BY THE CIA. THIS WAS DONE IN THE BELIEF THAT HE HAD INFORMATION THAT WOULD HELP LEAD TO THE CAPTURE OF OTHER AL-QA'IDA OPERATIVES THAT POSED SERIOUS THREATS--NOT THAT AL-MASRI POSED A THREAT, WHICH HAD BEEN THE STANDARD REQUIREMENT FOR DETAINMENT.

AFTER NATIONAL AGENCIES DISSENTED ON THE THREAT AL-MASRI POSED TO AMERICAN INTERESTS, THE NATIONAL SECURITY COUNCIL ENDED THE MATTER, CONCLUDING THAT HE SHOULD BE RELEASED AND THE GERMANS TOLD OF THE MATTER.

ON JULY 16, 2007, THE CIA INSPECTOR GENERAL'S REPORT STATED THAT "AVAILABLE INTELLIGENCE INFORMATION DID NOT PROVIDE A SUFFICIENT BASIS TO RENDER AND DETAIN KHALID AL-MASRI" AND HIS DETENTION WAS UNJUSTIFIED.

DUELING DECLARATIONS

SENATORS MITCH MCCONNELL AND SAXBY CHAMBLISS

"THE PROGRAM DEVELOPED SIGNIFICANT INTELLIGENCE THAT HELPED US IDENTIFY AND CAPTURE AL-QA'IDA TERRORISTS, DISRUPT THEIR ONGOING PLOTTING, AND TAKE DOWN USAMA BIN LADEN."

PRESIDENT OF AFGHANISTAN ASHRAF GHANI

"IT VIOLATED ALL ACCEPTED NORMS OF HUMAN RIGHTS IN THE WORLD."

PRESIDENT OBAMA

"MY LONG-HELD VIEW IS THAT THESE HARSH METHODS WERE NOT ONLY INCONSISTENT WITH OUR VALUES AS A NATION, THEY DID NOT SERVE OUR BROADER COUNTERTERRORISM EFFORTS OR OUR NATIONAL SECURITY INTERESTS."

END OF THE CIA'S DETENTION AND INTERROGATION PROGRAM

HASSAN GHUL, WHO WAS CAPTURED IN JAN-
UARY 2004 IN IRAQI KURDISTAN AND
PLACED IN CIA CUSTODY, GAVE AT LEAST 21
INTELLIGENCE REPORTS AND THE MOST
ACCURATE REPORTING ON THE FACILITATOR
WHO LED TO THE CAPTURE OF USAMA BIN
LADEN. ALL WITHOUT THE USE OF EITS! HE
ALSO PROVIDED INFORMATION RELATED TO
ABU MUSAB AL-ZARQAWI, ABU FARAJ AL-LIBI,
JAFFAR AL-TAYYAR AND A HOST OF OTHER
AL-QA'IDA LEADERS.

AND AS FAR AS SHARIF AL-MASRI IS CONCERNED . . .

BUT I'VE TOLD YOU EVERYTHING I KNOW!

SUBJECTED TO 59 HOURS OF SLEEP DEPRIVATION, GHUL EXPERIENCED HALLUCI-NATIONS THAT CONTIN-UED WHEN OTHER EITS WERE ADMINISTERED.

ON MAY 5, 2011, THE CIA LISTED GHUL ON A LIST OF DETAINEES SUBJECTED TO EITS WHO PROVIDED "TIER ONE" INFORMATION.

NOW ALL WE HAVE TO DO IS GET THE MAN.

IN JUNE 2004, A FOREIGN GOVERNMENT CAPTURED JANAT GUL, WHO,
BASED ON A CIA SOURCE, HAD INFORMATION ABOUT AL-QA'IDA'S PLANS
TO ATTACK THE UNITED STATES PRIOR TO THAT YEAR'S PRESIDENTIAL
ELECTION.

WITH GUL NOT YET IN THEIR CUSTODY, THE CIA SOUGHT AND RECEIVED
PERMISSION TO USE EITS, EXCEPT FOR WATERBOARDING, ON GUL FROM
THE NATIONAL SECURITY COUNCIL, WHICH INCLUDED VICE PRESIDENT
DICK CHENEY.

ONCE IN CIA CAPTIVITY, GUL WAS SUBJECTED TO MANY EITS, INCLUD-
ING SLEEP DEPRIVATION, FACIAL HOLDS, ATTENTION GRASPS, FACIAL
SLAPS, STRESS POSITIONS, AND WALLING.

BUT GUL NEVER GAVE ANY THREAT INFORMATION. EVENTUALLY HE WAS
TRANSFERRED TO FOREIGN GOVERNMENT CUSTODY AND RELEASED.

BY THE END OF 2004, THE VAST MAJORITY OF CIA DETAINEES—113 OF THE 119 IDENTIFIED IN THE COMMITTEE STUDY—HAD ALREADY ENTERED CIA CUSTODY. MOST WERE NO LONGER UNDERGOING ACTIVE INTERROGATION, BUT WERE INFREQUENTLY QUESTIONED AND AWAITING FINAL DISPOSITION. THE CIA TOOK ONLY SIX NEW DETAINEES BETWEEN JANUARY 2005 AND JANUARY 2009.

WHY DON'T THEY JUST LET ME GO?

THAT WOULD CERTAINLY MAKE MY LIFE A LOT EASIER.

THE CHIEF OF **DETENTION SITE BLACK** WROTE IN 2005 THAT BECAUSE OF THE LENGTH OF DETENTION OF DETAINEES IN CUSTODY, THEY "HAVE BEEN ALL BUT DRAINED OF ACTIONABLE INTELLIGENCE" AND THAT THEY NOW DEAL WITH "NATURAL AND PROGRESSIVE EFFECTS OF LONG-TERM SOLITARY CONFINEMENT OF DETAINEES."

ON MAY 10, 2005, THE ACTING ASSISTANT ATTORNEY GENERAL OF THE OFFICE OF LEGAL COUNSEL, STEVEN BRADBURY, ISSUED A LEGAL MEMORANDUM CONCLUDING THAT THE CIA'S USE OF EITS DID NOT VIOLATE THE TORTURE BAN.

I THOUGHT YOU TOLD ME THAT YOU'D LEAVE ME ALONE!

DURING MAY 2005, ABU FARAJ AL-LIBI, CONSIDERED THE THIRD MOST IMPORTANT PERSON IN AL-QA'IDA, WAS CAPTURED IN PAKISTAN AND DELIVERED TO THE CIA. BEGINNING ON MAY 28, THE CIA APPLIED EITS ON THE DETAINEE FOR MORE THAN A MONTH.

THE CIA CONTINUED TO INSIST AL-LIBI WAS WITHHOLDING IMPORTANT KNOWLEDGE, DESPITE THE FACT THAT HE HAD PROVIDED NO INFORMATION UNDER REPEATED AND EXTENSIVE USE OF EITS.

WHEN CIA MEDICAL OFFICERS EXPRESSED CONCERN ABOUT HIS HEALTH, THE USE OF EITS WAS DISCONTINUED.

WE KNOW IT'S FACTUAL, SIR. WE HAVE STATEMENTS FROM TOO MANY PEOPLE WHO VERIFY IT.

AND YOU'RE TELLING US THERE'S NOTHING WE CAN DO TO CHANGE YOUR MIND?

IN OCTOBER 2005, UPON LEARNING THAT *WASHINGTON POST* REPORTER DANA PRIEST HAD INFORMATION ABOUT THE CIA'S DETENTION AND INTERROGATION PROGRAM, THE CIA CONDUCTED NEGOTIATIONS WITH THE NEWSPAPER TO PREVENT THEIR PUBLISHING THE MATERIAL.

NO, THERE WAS NOTHING THEY COULD DO. THE ARTICLE WAS PRINTED WITH AMAZING RESULTS.

ONE [REDACTED COUNTRY] DEMANDED THE CLOSURE OF CIA **DETENTION SITE BLACK** AND THE TRANSFERAL OF ALL PRISONERS.

REMEMBER, YOU CANNOT USE TORTURE!

AND YOU CANNOT INFORM THE U.S. AMBASSADOR THAT WE ARE HERE!

YOU THINK THEY ARE SENDING US HOME?

OH, YES! AND FILLING OUR POCKETS WITH GOLD!

AT ONE POINT, ALL CIA DETAINEES WERE LOCATED IN [REDACTED COUNTRY] UNTIL NEW ARRANGEMENTS COULD BE MADE WITH SEVERAL OTHERS.

LOOKS LIKE THE SO-CALLED DETAINEES HAVE ARRIVED.

IN 2005 AND 2006, THE CIA TRANSFERRED DETAINEES TO AT LEAST NINE UNNAMED COUNTRIES AS WELL AS TO THE U.S. MILITARY IN IRAQ.

-44-

I DIRECTED OUR GOVERNMENT'S SENIOR NATIONAL SECURITY OFFICERS TO DO EVERYTHING IN THEIR POWER . . .

ON SEPTEMBER 6, 2006, PRESIDENT BUSH DELIVERED A SPEECH ACKNOWLEDGING THAT THE NATION HAD HELD AL-QA'IDA OPERATIVES IN SECRET DETENTION, THAT THE CIA HAD USED AN "ALTERNATIVE SET OF PROCEDURES" IN QUESTIONING THE DETAINEES, AND THEN DESCRIBED INFORMATION OBTAINED FROM DETAINEES.

THE PART OF THE SPEECH BASED ON CIA INFORMATION CONTAINED SIGNIFICANT INACCURACIES.

THOSE HELD AT GUANTANAMO INCLUDE SUSPECTED BOMB MAKERS, TERRORIST TRAINERS, RECRUITERS AND FACILITATORS, AND POTENTIAL SUICIDE BOMBERS!

AND THEY FORCED ME TO STAND THERE NUDE WITH MY ARMS SHACKLED OVER MY HEAD AND . . .

IN THE SPEECH, THE PRESIDENT ANNOUNCED THE TRANSFER OF 14 DETAINEES TO DEPARTMENT OF DEFENSE CUSTODY AT GUANTANAMO BAY AND THE SUBMISSION OF PROPOSED LEGISLATION ON MILITARY COMMISSIONS TO CONGRESS.

AS ALL DETAINEES IN CIA CUSTODY HAD BEEN TRANSFERRED TO OTHER NATIONS, THE CIA HAD NO DETAINEES IN CUSTODY AT THE TIME.

IN OCTOBER 2006, THE ICRC WAS ALLOWED TO MEET WITH THE 14 DETAINEES IN GUANTANAMO BAY. THEIR REPORT CONCLUDED THAT "THE ICRC CLEARLY CONSIDERS THAT THE ALLEGATIONS OF THE 14 INCLUDE . . . [TREATMENT] THAT AMOUNTED TO TORTURE AND/OR CRUEL, INHUMAN OR DEGRADING TREATMENT."

COMITE INTERNATIONAL GENEVE

ICRC

EFFECTIVENESS OF THE CIA'S EITS

IN JUNE 2006, THE ADMINISTRATION DETERMINED THAT NEW LEGISLATION WAS NEEDED TO CONTINUE USE OF EITS. AFTER MUCH DELIBERATION, IN JULY 2007, SLEEP DEPRIVATION, DIETARY MANIPULATION, FACIAL GRASP, FACIAL SLAP, ABDOMINAL SLAP, AND THE ATTENTION GRASP WERE DEEMED ACCEPTABLE; NUDITY, SHACKLED IN STANDING POSITION, WALLING, AND WATERBOARDING WERE BANNED.

I TELL YOU I KNOW NOTHING!

ON JUNE 25, 2007, AL-QA'IDA FACILITATOR MUHAMMAD RAHIM WAS CAPTURED IN PAKISTAN AND RENDERED INTO CIA CUSTODY IN [REDACTED COUNTRY]. IN JULY, BELIEVING HE HAD WORKED DIRECTLY WITH USAMA BIN LADEN AND AYMAN AL-ZAWAHIRI, INTERROGATORS "EMPLOYED INTERROGATION MEASURES OF FACIAL SLAP, ABDOMINAL SLAP, AND FACIAL HOLD" AND INTENDED TO DO SO UNTIL HE WOULD GIVE THEM INFORMATION.

OH, YES, BIN LADEN HAS A SECRET HOME IN MIAMI WHERE HE OCCASIONALLY LIVES WITH FIVE, NO, SIX AMERICAN BEAUTIES . . .

RAHIM THREATENED TO FABRICATE INFORMATION AS HE WAS SUBJECTED TO EIGHT EXTENSIVE SLEEP DEPRIVATION SESSIONS, SHACKLED IN A STANDING POSITION WEARING A DIAPER AND A PAIR OF SHORTS, AND RESTRICTED TO AN ALMOST COMPLETELY LIQUID DIET.

I'M EXHAUSTED, CAN YOU NOT SEE?

FINALLY, IN SEPTEMBER 2007, MUHAMMAD RAHIM WAS LEFT IN HIS CELL WITH MINIMAL CONTACT WITH CIA PERSONNEL FOR APPROXIMATELY SIX WEEKS. BUT EITS WERE ONCE AGAIN TRIED BETWEEN NOVEMBER 2 AND NOVEMBER 8, 2007, THIS TIME WITH 138.5 HOURS OF SLEEP DEPRIVATION AND DIETARY MANIPULATION.

HERE! HE'S YOURS.

GUANTANAMO

WITH OUR PLEASURE!

YOU ARE FROM PAKISTAN, YES?

NO, SIR, I WAS BORN IN AFGHANISTAN.

THE DETENTION AND INTERROGATION OF RAHIM RESULTED IN NO DISSEMINATED INTELLIGENCE REPORTS. HE WAS FINALLY RENDERED TO U.S. MILITARY CUSTODY AT GUANTANAMO BAY.

ON APRIL 21 AND 22, 2008, THE CIA CONVENED AN AFTER-ACTION REVIEW OF THEIR INTERROGATION OF RAHIM IN AN ATTEMPT TO LEARN WHY IT DID NOT SUCCEED. FIRST, THEY DECIDED IT WAS THE INTERROGATION TEAM'S LACK OF KNOWLEDGE OF THE MAN.

THEY THEN BLAMED THE DECISION TO USE EITS IMMEDIATELY AFTER THE SHORT "NEUTRAL PROBE" AND ISOLATION PERIOD.

THEY ALSO CITED THE LACK OF CLARITY ABOUT WHETHER THE NONCOERCIVE TECHNIQUES DESCRIBED IN THE ARMY FIELD MANUAL WERE PERMITTED, THE TEAM'S INABILITY TO CONFRONT RAHIM WITH INCRIMINATING EVIDENCE, AND THE USE OF MULTIPLE IMPROVISED INTERROGATION APPROACHES.

BUT THIS REVIEW WAS FOR NAUGHT. RAHIM WAS THE LAST CIA DETAINEE IN THE DETENTION AND INTERROGATION PROGRAM.

WHY DO WE COME UP WITH THESE IDEAS NOW?

YES, WHEN IT'S TIME TO PACK UP AND GO HOME.

TWO CIA CONTRACTORS WHO HAD PLAYED CENTRAL ROLES IN THE DEVELOPMENT OF THE CIA'S EITS IN 2002 AND THEN USED THOSE TECHNIQUES AS CONTRACT INTERROGATORS, FORMED A PRIVATE COMPANY IN 2005.

THANK GOODNESS THEY DIDN'T REQUEST OPERATIONAL MASSEUSES.

PAPERS ARE SIGNED AND THEY'RE IN BUSINESS!

COMPANY Y, IN ADDITION TO PROVIDING INTERROGATORS TO THE CIA, WAS GRANTED A SOLE-SOURCE CONTRACT TO PROVIDE OPERATIONAL PSYCHOLOGISTS, DEBRIEFERS, AND SECURITY PERSONNEL AT CIA DETENTION SITES.

GLAD THEY'RE KEEPING THINGS IN THE CIA FAMILY!

BY 2006, THE VALUE OF THE BASE CONTRACT FOR COMPANY Y WAS IN EXCESS OF $180 MILLION. AS OF MAY 2007, COMPANY Y HAD HIRED A [REDACTED AMOUNT] OF FORMER CIA OFFICERS, MANY OF WHOM HAD BEEN INVOLVED WITH THE CIA'S DETENTION AND INTERROGATION PROGRAM. UNDER THE CIA'S INDEMNIFICATION CONTRACT, THE CIA IS OBLIGATED TO PAY COMPANY Y'S LEGAL EXPENSES THROUGH 2021.

ON DECEMBER 5, 2007, CONGRESS PASSED AN AMENDMENT THAT BANNED COERCIVE INTERROGATION TECHNIQUES AND ESTABLISHED THE ARMY FIELD MANUAL AS THE STANDARD FOR ALL GOVERNMENT INTERROGATIONS. HOWEVER, PRESIDENT BUSH VETOED THE MEASURE AND IN A RADIO ADDRESS SAID . . .

THE BILL CONGRESS SENT ME WOULD TAKE AWAY ONE OF THE MOST VALUABLE TOOLS IN THE WAR ON TERROR: THE CIA PROGRAM TO DETAIN AND QUESTION KEY TERRORIST LEADERS AND OPERATIVES . . . TO RESTRICT THE CIA TO METHODS IN THE ARMY FIELD MANUAL . . . COULD COST AMERICAN LIVES.

THE PRESIDENT'S DECLARATIONS REGARDING THE ROLE OF THE CIA'S TECHNIQUES WERE NEARLY ENTIRELY INACCURATE.

ON MARCH 11, 2008, BY A VOTE OF 225–188, THE HOUSE FAILED TO OVERRIDE THE VETO.

IN DECEMBER 2008 AND JANUARY 2009, CIA OFFICERS BRIEFED NEWLY ELECTED PRESIDENT BARACK OBAMA'S TRANSITION TEAM ON THE CIA'S DETENTION AND INTERROGATION PROGRAM. CIA DIRECTOR MICHAEL HAYDEN PREPARED A STATEMENT THAT SAID . . .

DESPITE WHAT YOU HAVE HEARD OR READ IN A VARIETY OF PUBLIC FORA, THESE ENHANCED INTERROGATION TECHNIQUES AND THIS PROGRAM DID WORK.

THE PREPARED MATERIAL INCLUDED INACCURATE INFORMATION ON THE OPERATION AND MANAGEMENT OF THE PROGRAM.

ON JANUARY 22, 2009, PRESIDENT OBAMA ISSUED EXECUTIVE ORDER 13491, WHICH REQUIRED THE CIA TO "CLOSE AS EXPEDITIOUSLY AS POSSIBLE ANY DETENTION FACILITIES THAT IT CURRENTLY OPERATES AND . . . [SHALL] NOT OPERATE ANY SUCH DETENTION FACILITY IN THE FUTURE." THE EXECUTIVE ORDER PROHIBITED ANY U.S. GOVERNMENT EMPLOYEE FROM USING INTERROGATION TECHNIQUES OTHER THAN THOSE IN THE ARMY FIELD MANUAL 2–22.3 ON HUMAN INTELLIGENCE COLLECTION OPERATIONS.

THESE TECHNIQUES HAVE SAVED LIVES, DISRUPTED TERRORIST PLOTS, HELPED PREVENT A SUBSEQUENT ATTACK ON OUR COUNTRY, CAPTURED TERRORISTS, AND COLLECTED CRITICAL INTELLIGENCE THAT COULD NOT HAVE OCCURRED IN ANY OTHER WAY!

FROM 2002 TO 2009, IN ORDER TO OBTAIN POLICY AUTHORIZATION AND LEGAL APPROVALS, THE CIA MADE A SERIES OF REPRESENTATIONS TO THE WHITE HOUSE ASSUMING THAT THE EITS PRODUCED INTELLIGENCE THAT COULD NOT BE GAINED ANY OTHER WAY.

AS YOU WELL KNOW, IT WAS A NECESSITY TO ACCOMPLISH OUR TASK AND IT SAVED THOUSANDS OF LIVES!

DURING THE PERIOD THE INTERROGATION PROGRAM WAS OPERATIONAL, THERE WERE THREE REVIEWS ADDRESSING ITS EFFECTS. EACH OF THEM RELIED ONLY ON INTERVIEWS WITH CIA PERSONNEL INVOLVED IN THE PROCESS OR PREPARED BY THEM. NO INDEPENDENT AUTHORITY EVER VALIDATED THE CLAIMED INTELLIGENCE, NO REVIEW EVER ASCERTAINED THE SUPPOSED TIME THE DECLARATION OCCURRED OR IF THE INFORMATION WAS OTHERWISE UNKNOWN.

BEFORE THE CIA TOOK CUSTODY OF ITS FIRST DETAINEE, CIA ATTORNEYS RESEARCHED THE LIMITS OF COERCIVE INTERROGATIONS AND LEGAL DEFINITIONS OF "TORTURE." THEY CAME UP WITH BOTH THE "NECESSITY" DEFENSE AND THE DECLARATION THAT IT "SAVED MANY LIVES"!

AND YET, ON JUNE 26, 2003, PRESIDENT BUSH ISSUED A STATEMENT FOR THE UNITED NATIONS INTERNATIONAL DAY IN SUPPORT OF VICTIMS OF TORTURE, SAYING: "THE UNITED STATES IS COMMITTED TO THE WORLDWIDE ELIMINATION OF TORTURE AND WE ARE LEADING THE FIGHT BY EXAMPLE!"

THE PRESIDENT'S STATEMENT CAUSED CONCERN AMONG MANY ADMINISTRATION OFFICERS. GEORGE TENET, DIRECTOR OF THE CIA, SENT A MEMO TO NATIONAL SECURITY ADVISOR CONDOLEEZZA RICE STATING . . .

> RECENT ADMINISTRATION RESPONSES TO INQUIRIES . . . ABOUT THE ADMINISTRATION'S POSITION HAVE CREATED THE IMPRESSION THAT THESE TECHNIQUES ARE NOT USED BY U.S. PERSONNEL AND ARE NO LONGER APPROVED.

THIS ALSO PROMPTED THE CIA TO PROVIDE ADDITIONAL INFORMATION ABOUT THE "EFFECTIVENESS" OF THE ENHANCED TECHNIQUES, THE "THWARTING" OF SPECIFIC PLOTS, AND THE CAPTURE OF SPECIFIC TERRORISTS. ALL ALMOST ENTIRELY INACCURATE.

THE CIA PROVIDED BRIEFING SLIDES CLAIMING THAT EITS WERE ESSENTIAL TO IDENTIFYING AL-QA'IDA FIGURES SUCH AS IYMAN FARIS, MAJID KHAN, SAYF AL-RAHMAN PARACHA, JOSÉ PADILLA, AND RICHARD REID, AS WELL AS INFORMATION ON "ATTACKS ON BANKS, SUBWAYS, PETROLEUM, AND AIRCRAFT INDUSTRIES." ALL INACCURATE!

ON SEPTEMBER 6, 2006, PRESIDENT BUSH DELIVERED A WELL-DISCUSSED AND PREPARED SPEECH SUPPORTING THE USE OF THE CIA'S EITS AND ITS SUPPOSED SUCCESSES. PART OF THAT SPEECH STATED . . .

> ONCE IN OUR CUSTODY, KSM WAS QUESTIONED BY THE CIA USING THESE PROCEDURES AND HE SOON PROVIDED INFORMATION THAT HELPED US STOP ANOTHER PLANNED ATTACK ON THE UNITED STATES.

THE SPEECH AND ITS ASSUMPTIONS WERE CHALLENGED IN MANY PLACES BY THE *NEW YORK TIMES* AND BY RON SUSSKIND IN *TIME* MAGAZINE. THE FALSE INFORMATION INCLUDED IN THE SPEECH HAS BEEN REPEATED IN NUMEROUS ARTICLES, BOOKS, AND BROADCASTS.

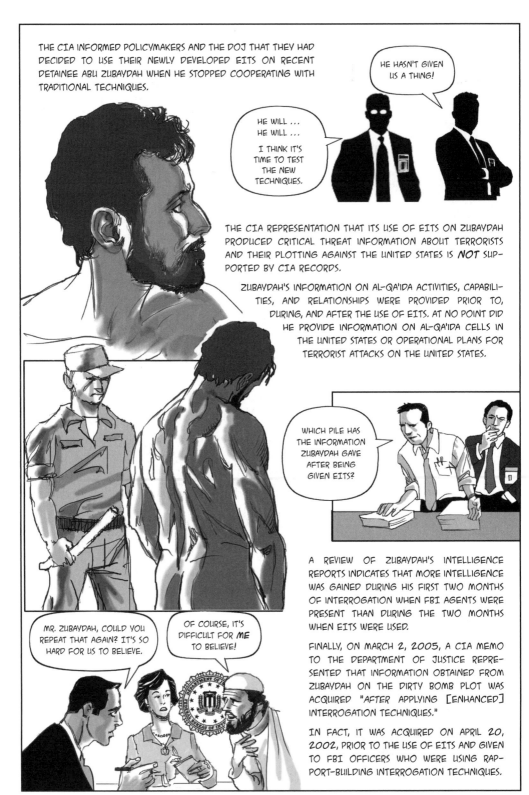

THE CIA INFORMED POLICYMAKERS AND THE DOJ THAT THEY HAD DECIDED TO USE THEIR NEWLY DEVELOPED EITS ON RECENT DETAINEE ABU ZUBAYDAH WHEN HE STOPPED COOPERATING WITH TRADITIONAL TECHNIQUES.

HE HASN'T GIVEN US A THING!

HE WILL ... HE WILL ...

I THINK IT'S TIME TO TEST THE NEW TECHNIQUES.

THE CIA REPRESENTATION THAT ITS USE OF EITS ON ZUBAYDAH PRODUCED CRITICAL THREAT INFORMATION ABOUT TERRORISTS AND THEIR PLOTTING AGAINST THE UNITED STATES IS **NOT** SUPPORTED BY CIA RECORDS.

ZUBAYDAH'S INFORMATION ON AL-QA'IDA ACTIVITIES, CAPABILITIES, AND RELATIONSHIPS WERE PROVIDED PRIOR TO, DURING, AND AFTER THE USE OF EITS. AT NO POINT DID HE PROVIDE INFORMATION ON AL-QA'IDA CELLS IN THE UNITED STATES OR OPERATIONAL PLANS FOR TERRORIST ATTACKS ON THE UNITED STATES.

WHICH PILE HAS THE INFORMATION ZUBAYDAH GAVE AFTER BEING GIVEN EITS?

MR. ZUBAYDAH, COULD YOU REPEAT THAT AGAIN? IT'S SO HARD FOR US TO BELIEVE.

OF COURSE, IT'S DIFFICULT FOR **ME** TO BELIEVE!

A REVIEW OF ZUBAYDAH'S INTELLIGENCE REPORTS INDICATES THAT MORE INTELLIGENCE WAS GAINED DURING HIS FIRST TWO MONTHS OF INTERROGATION WHEN FBI AGENTS WERE PRESENT THAN DURING THE TWO MONTHS WHEN EITS WERE USED.

FINALLY, ON MARCH 2, 2005, A CIA MEMO TO THE DEPARTMENT OF JUSTICE REPRESENTED THAT INFORMATION OBTAINED FROM ZUBAYDAH ON THE DIRTY BOMB PLOT WAS ACQUIRED "AFTER APPLYING [ENHANCED] INTERROGATION TECHNIQUES."

IN FACT, IT WAS ACQUIRED ON APRIL 20, 2002, PRIOR TO THE USE OF EITS AND GIVEN TO FBI OFFICERS WHO WERE USING RAPPORT-BUILDING INTERROGATION TECHNIQUES.

REGARDING THE INTERROGATION OF KHALID SHAYKH MOHAMMAD (KSM), REPRESENTATIONS MADE BY THE CIA TO THE OIG, THE WHITE HOUSE, THE DEPARTMENT OF JUSTICE, AND THE AMERICAN PUBLIC INCLUDED THE FOLLOWING:

1. KSM PROVIDED LITTLE INFORMATION OF ANY USE PRIOR TO THE USE OF EITS.
2. THE CIA OVERCAME KSM'S RESISTANCE THROUGH THESE TECHNIQUES.
3. THE WATERBOARDING TECHNIQUE WAS PARTICULARLY EFFECTIVE.
4. KSM "RECANTED LITTLE OF THE INFORMATION" AND HE WAS "GENERALLY ACCURATE" AND "CONSISTENT."
5. HE INDICATED AN ATTACK WAS IMMINENT UPON HIS ARREST.

TO THE CONTRARY, MULTIPLE CIA RECORDS DESCRIBE THE INEFFECTIVENESS OF EITS IN GAINING KSM'S COOPERATION.

THE GENERAL U.S. POPULATION IS WEAK, LACKS RESILIENCE, AND WOULD BE UNABLE TO DO WHAT IS NECESSARY.

THERE ARE NO CIA OPERATIONAL OR INTERROGATION RECORDS TO SUPPORT THE REPRESENTATION THAT KSM AND ABU ZUBAYDAH MADE THIS STATEMENT.

GENERAL HAYDEN, OF THE 8,000 INTELLIGENCE REPORTS THAT WERE PROVIDED, AS YOU SAID, BY 30 OF THE DETAINEES--

BY ALL 97, MA'AM.

SENATOR SNOWE

THE CIA CLAIMED THAT EITS RESULTED IN THE COLLECTION OF "A HIGH VOLUME OF CRITICAL INTELLIGENCE" ON AL-QA'IDA. IN APRIL 2007, CIA DIRECTOR MICHAEL HAYDEN TESTIFIED THAT ITS INTERROGATION PROGRAM IS "THE MOST SUCCESSFUL PROGRAM BEING CONDUCTED BY AMERICAN INTELLIGENCE TODAY."

HIS STATEMENT IS NOT SUPPORTED BY CIA RECORDS. RECORDS REVEAL THAT 34% OF THE 119 DETAINEES PRODUCED NO REPORTS, NEARLY 70% PRODUCED FEWER THAN 15, AND OF THE 39 SUBJECTED TO EITS, NEARLY 20% PRODUCED NO REPORTS WHILE 40% PRODUCED FEWER THAN 15. FIVE DETAINEES PRODUCED MORE THAN 40% OF ALL REPORTING AND TWO OF THE FIVE WERE NOT SUBJECTED TO EITS.

FROM 2003 TO 2009, THE CIA REPEATEDLY REPRESENTED THAT EITS WERE EFFECTIVE AND NECESSARY TO PRODUCE CRITICAL INTELLIGENCE ENABLING "THE CIA TO DISRUPT TERRORIST PLOTS, CAPTURE ADDITIONAL TERRORISTS, AND COLLECT A HIGH VOLUME OF CRITICAL INTELLIGENCE ON AL-QA'IDA."

THE SENATE COMMITTEE INVESTIGATED EIGHT OF THE MOST FREQUENTLY CITED EXAMPLES OF "THWARTED PLOTS." THE COMMITTEE FOUND THE CIA'S REPRESENTATIONS TO BE INACCURATE AND UNSUPPORTED BY CIA RECORDS.

NO, I DO NOT KNOW THEIR NAMES, BUT I KNOW THERE ARE TWO OF THEM.

THE CIA REPRESENTED THAT ITS ENHANCED TECHNIQUES PRODUCED CRITICAL AND OTHERWISE UNAVAILABLE INTELLIGENCE LEADING TO THE CAPTURE OF JOSÉ PADILLA. THIS WAS INACCURATE.

THE CIA FIRST RECEIVED WORD ON THE TERRORIST THREAT POSED BY PADILLA FROM ABU ZUBAYDAH, WHO, PRIOR TO BEING SUBJECTED TO EITS, PROVIDED INFORMATION ON TERRORIST PLOTTING BY TWO INDIVIDUALS.

DON'T ANY **ONE** OF YOU MAKE A MOVE!

THE THWARTING OF THE KARACHI PLOT (A PLAN TO TARGET A VARIETY OF UNITED STATES AND WESTERN INTERESTS IN THE KARACHI AREA) IS ANOTHER OF THE EIGHT MOST FREQUENTLY CITED EXAMPLES BY THE CIA AS EVIDENCE OF THE IMPORTANCE OF EITS. THESE REPRESENTATIONS WERE INACCURATE.

THE KARACHI PLOT WAS DISRUPTED BY PAKISTANI AUTHORITIES WITH THE CONFISCATION OF EXPLOSIVES AND THE ARRESTS OF AMMAR AL-BALUCHI AND KHALLAD BIN ATTASH IN APRIL 2003, UNRELATED TO ANY REPORTING FROM THE CIA.

AND OUR DISCOVERY OF THE KARACHI PLOT COULD NOT HAVE OCCURRED WITHOUT OUR CAREFUL USAGE OF THE ENHANCED INTERROGATION TECHNIQUES.

THE CIA ALSO PROVIDED THE "DISCOVERY" AND/OR THE "THWARTING" OF THE "SECOND WAVE" PLOT (TWO EFFORTS BY KSM TO STRIKE AMERICA'S WEST COAST WITH AIRPLANES) AND THE "DISCOVERY" OF THE AL-GHURABA GROUP AS EVIDENCE OF THE EFFECTIVENESS OF EITS.

THIS, TOO, WAS INACCURATE. A REVIEW OF CIA CABLES AND OTHER DOCUMENTS FOUND THE CIA'S EITS PLAYED NO ROLE IN THE THWARTING OF THE SECOND WAVE PLOT NOR IN THE DISCOVERY OF A 17-MEMBER "CELL TASKED WITH EXECUTING THE 'SECOND WAVE.'"

THE CIA PROVIDED THE CAPTURE OF DHIREN BAROT, AKA ISSA AL-HINDI, AND THE THWARTING OF BAROT'S UNITED KINGDOM URBAN TARGETS PLOT AS EVIDENCE OF THE EFFECTIVENESS OF ITS ENHANCED TECHNIQUES.

THESE REPRESENTATIONS ARE INACCURATE. THE OPERATION THAT RESULTED IN THE IDENTIFICATION OF AL-HINDI AS BAROT, BAROT'S ARREST, AND THE THWARTING OF HIS PLOT RESULTED FROM INVESTIGATIVE ACTIVITIES OF U.K. GOVERNMENT AUTHORITIES.

LOOK WHAT I'VE DISCOVERED HERE!

THE CIA PROVIDED THE IDENTIFICATION, ARREST, CAPTURE, INVESTIGATION, AND PROSECUTION OF IYMAN FARIS AS EVIDENCE OF THE EFFECTIVENESS OF EITS.

THESE CLAIMS WERE INACCURATE. FARIS WAS IDENTIFIED, INVESTIGATED, AND LINKED DIRECTLY TO AL-QA'IDA PRIOR TO ANY MENTION OF HIS NAME BY KSM, AND KNOWN TO THE INTELLIGENCE COMMUNITY EVEN BEFORE THE 9/11 ATTACKS. AN OHIO-BASED TRUCK DRIVER, HE WAS QUIZZED BY KSM ABOUT CUTTING SUSPENSION CABLES ON THE BROOKLYN BRIDGE AND DECLINED TO PARTICIPATE.

THE CIA PROVIDED THE IDENTIFICATION, DISCOVERY, CAPTURE, AND ARREST OF SAJID BADAT, THE ACCOMPLICE OF "SHOE BOMBER" RICHARD REID IN HIS FAILED ATTEMPT TO DESTROY A PLANE ON ITS FLIGHT TO THE UNITED STATES, AS EVIDENCE OF THE EFFECTIVENESS OF EITS.

THESE REPRESENTATIONS WERE INACCURATE. ACCORDING TO THE UNITED KINGDOM'S OWN INVESTIGATIVE SUMMARY--AS WELL AS OTHER CIA RECORDS--THE INVESTIGATION OF BADAT WAS A U.K.-LED INVESTIGATION AND UNRELATED TO INFORMATION FROM CIA DETAINEES.

THE CIA CLAIMED THAT THE IDENTIFICATION AND THWARTING OF THE HEATHROW AIRPORT AND CANARY WHARF PLOTS WERE RESULTS OF EITS.

THESE REPRESENTATIONS WERE INACCURATE. THE PLANS TO HIGHJACK A COMMERCIAL AIRCRAFT AND BOMB LONDON'S FAMED AIRPORT AND A BUILDING IN A MAJOR BUSINESS DISTRICT HAD BEEN FULLY DISRUPTED BEFORE ANY OF THOSE TECHNIQUES WERE EVER USED.

THE CIA CLAIMED THAT EFFECTIVE USE OF EITS ON KSM PROVIDED THE "FIRST" INFORMATION ON A MONEY TRANSFER BY MAJID KHAN THAT LED TO THE CAPTURE OF HAMBALI.

HOWEVER, CIA RECORDS INDICATE THAT INTELLIGENCE FROM A CIA SOURCE, THAI INVESTIGATIVE ACTIV-ITIES IN THAILAND, AND PURE LUCK LED TO HAMBALI'S CAPTURE. THAI AGENTS STUMBLED ON THE CIA'S NUMBER ONE TARGET IN SOUTH-EAST ASIA WHILE HE WAS GIVING AN INTERVIEW. OH, YES . . . WITH THE CIA'S ORAL HISTORY PROGRAM.

EXCUSE ME, BUT WOULDN'T YOU BE . . .

STOP! STOP!

I'LL TELL YOU WHO WAS BEHIND THE 9/11 RAIDS!

BESIDES THESE EIGHT MOST-IMPORTANT PLOTS, THE SSCI FOUND AND EXAMINED 12 OTHER LESS-FREQUENTLY CITED EXAMPLES USED TO JUSTIFY THE USE OF EITS.

ON AT LEAST TWO OCCASIONS, THE CIA REPRESENTED INACCURATELY THAT ABU ZUBAYDAH PROVIDED THE FIRST INFORMATION THAT KSM MASTERMINDED THE 9/11 ATTACKS AFTER FACING EITS. THE INFORMATION OBTAINED FROM ZUBAYDAH WAS CORROBORATIVE; THE INTEL WAS ALREADY IN CIA DATABASES.

THE CIA REPRESENTED THAT ZUBAYDAH PROVIDED "IMPORTANT" AND "VITAL" INFORMATION BY IDENTIFYING KSM'S ALIAS "MUKHTAR" AFTER USE OF EITS.

WHILE ZUBAYDAH DID PROVIDE THIS INFORMATION, HE DID SO TO FBI INTERROGATORS PRIOR TO THE START OF THE ENHANCED PROGRAM. AT THE TIME, HE WAS STILL IN INTENSIVE CARE AT A HOSPITAL RECOVERING FROM A GUNSHOT WOUND. EVEN THEN, IT WAS CORROBORATIVE EVIDENCE.

I DON'T KNOW IF YOU KNOW THIS, BUT...

THE CIA REPRESENTED THAT INTELLIGENCE DERIVED FROM THE USE OF EITS THWARTED PLOTS AGAINST U.S. MILITARY BASE CAMP LEMONNIER IN DJIBOUTI. THESE REPRESENTATIONS WERE INACCURATE. DEFENDING THE USE OF EITS ON SEPTEMBER 6, 2006, THE PRESIDENT DECLARED . . .

THIS IS INTELLIGENCE THAT CANNOT BE FOUND ANY OTHER PLACE. AND OUR SECURITY DEPENDS ON GETTING THIS KIND OF INFORMATION.

ACCOMPANYING THE PRESIDENT'S SPEECH, AN OFFICE OF NATIONAL INTELLIGENCE RELEASE STATED, "THE CIA DESIGNED A NEW INTERROGATION PROGRAM THAT WOULD BE SAFE, EFFECTIVE, AND LEGAL."

ON OCTOBER 30, 2007, A CIA PRESENTATION STATED THAT THIS PROGRAM WAS "CRITICAL TO [THE CIA'S] ABILITY TO PROTECT THE AMERICAN HOMELAND AND U.S. FORCES AND CITIZENS ABROAD FROM TERRORIST ATTACKS." A U.S. INFORMANT, THEY CLAIMED, TOLD THEM . . .

HE WON'T NEED ANY OF THE TECHNIQUES, JUST THE FASTEST STENOGRAPHER WE HAVE!

AN OPERATION IS UNDERWAY TO ATTACK THE U.S. MILITARY AT CAMP LEMONNIER IN DJIBOUTI.

A REVIEW OF CIA RECORDS FOUND THAT THE DETAINEE TO WHOM CIA RECORDS REFER, GULEED HASSAN DOURAD, WAS *NOT* SUBJECTED TO EITS AND THAT THE CIA WAS AWARE OF AND REPORTED THE TERRORIST THREAT PRIOR TO RECEIVING WORD FROM DOURAD . . .

NEITHER THE DETENTION OF DOURAD NOR THE INFORMATION HE PROVIDED THWARTED A TERRORIST PLOT AGAINST CAMP LEMONNIER. AND CIA RECORDS INDICATE THAT ATTACK PLANNING AGAINST THE CAMP CONTINUED TO A DATE BEYOND THE PRESIDENT'S SPEECH IN 2006.

BUT BY THE END OF DECEMBER 2003, DJIBOUTIAN AUTHORITIES CONFIRMED THAT DOURAD HAD CASED CAMP LEMONNIER AND APPEARED TO HAVE "FORMULATED A COMPLETE TARGETING PACKAGE, WHICH INCLUDED AN ESCAPE ROUTE." IT WAS THIS REPORTING THAT LED TO DOURAD'S CAPTURE ON MARCH 4, 2004.

I THINK IT'S THE SAME GUY WHO'S HUNG AROUND HERE BEFORE.

IN ADDITION TO CIA CLAIMS THAT INFORMATION PRODUCED DURING OR AFTER THE USE OF EITS LED TO THE DISRUPTION OF TERRORIST PLOTS AND THE CAPTURE OF TERRORISTS, THE CIA ALSO REPRESENTED IT WAS NECESSARY TO VALIDATE SOURCES. THIS WAS BASED ON ONE CIA DETAINEE, JANAT GUL, CONTRADICTING THE REPORTING OF ANOTHER CIA DETAINEE.

> DETAINEE INFORMATION IS A KEY TOOL FOR VALIDATING CLANDESTINE SOURCES.

> IN ONE CASE, THE DETAINEE'S INFORMATION PROVED TO BE THE ACCURATE STORY, AND THE CLANDESTINE SOURCE WAS CONFRONTED AND . . . ADMITTED TO EMBELLISHING.

> ARE WE EXPECTED TO BELIEVE EVERYTHING WRITTEN HERE?

IN JANUARY 2009, THE CIA COMPILED A BRIEFING BOOK FOR THE INCOMING OBAMA ADMINISTRATION THAT INCLUDED "PAKISTAN-BASED FACILITATOR JANAT GUL'S MOST SIGNIFICANT REPORTING HELPED [TO] INVALIDATE A CIA ASSET WHO WAS PROVIDING INFORMATION ABOUT THE 2004 PRE-ELECTION THREAT."

THE CIA'S REPRESENTATIONS DID NOT DESCRIBE HOW THE ASSET'S REPORTING WAS ALREADY DOUBTED PRIOR TO THE USE OF EITS ON GUL.

NOR THAT THE CIA HAD CONCLUDED THAT GUL WAS NOT A HIGH-LEVEL AL-QA'IDA FIGURE AND DID NOT POSSESS THREAT INFORMATION.

GUL WAS CAPTURED IN [REDACTED COUNTRY] IN JUNE 2004 AND RENDERED TO CIA CUSTODY. THOUGH THE USE OF EITS WERE SUSPENDED BY THE CIA, THE AGENCY REQUESTED AND WAS GRANTED THE RIGHTS TO USE THEM ON GUL TO HELP EVALUATE THE THREAT REPORTING OF AN **ASSET Y**.

> ARE YOU SURE THIS IS NECESSARY?

PRIOR TO THE USE OF THE EN-
HANCED TECHNIQUES, JANAT GUL
DENIED ANY KNOWLEDGE OF . . .

ON AUGUST 25, THE CIA ASSOCIATE
GENERAL COUNSEL ASSERTED THAT
GUL'S "RESISTANCE INCREASES WHEN
QUESTIONED ABOUT MATTERS THAT
MAY CONNECT HIM TO AL-QA'IDA OR
EVIDENCE . . . OF OPERATIONAL TER-
RORIST ACTIVITIES." HE THEN RE-
QUESTED APPROVAL FOR THE USE OF
FOUR ENHANCED TECHNIQUES TO BE
USED AGAINST GUL . . .

HOWEVER, ONLY FOUR DAYS LATER,
ON AUGUST 31, THE CIA'S ASSOCI-
ATE GENERAL COUNSEL OBJECTED
TO THE USE OF EITS AND WROTE,
"DESPITE THESE CONCERNS, ON
SEPTEMBER 7, 2004, CIA HEAD-
QUARTERS EXTENDED APPROVAL
FOR 30 DAYS OF SLEEP
DEPRIVATION. THOUGH GUL
WAS NOT SUBJECTED TO
ANY ENHANCED TECH-
NIQUES FROM THEN ON."

THE CIA REPRESENTED THAT INFORMATION GAINED THROUGH THE USE OF EITS PRODUCED OTHERWISE UNAVAILABLE INTELLIGENCE THAT LED TO THE IDENTIFICATION AND/OR ARREST OF UZHAIR PARACHA AND HIS FATHER SAIFULLAH PARACHA. THESE REPRESENTATIONS INCLUDE INACCURATE INFORMATION AND OMIT SIGNIFICANT INFORMATION THAT PREVIOUSLY LINKED THE PARACHAS TO AL-QA'IDA RELATED ACTIVITIES.

YES! I'LL TELL YOU EVERYTHING I KNOW!

YOU HAVEN'T LET ME SLEEP FOR FOUR DAYS! I'M EXHAUSTED!

THEN TELL US ABOUT THE SMUGGLING PLOT!

CIA REPRESENTATIONS ALSO CREDIT THE USE OF EITS ON THE PARACHAS WITH THE IDENTIFICATION OF A PLOT TO SMUGGLE EXPLOSIVES INTO THE UNITED STATES.

CIA RECORDS INDICATE THE PLOT WAS DENIED BY THE SUPPOSED PARTICIPANTS, AND AT LEAST ONE SENIOR COUNTERTERRORISM OFFICIAL QUESTIONED THE PLAUSIBILITY OF THIS GIVEN THE EASE OF ACQUIRING EXPLOSIVE MATERIAL INSIDE THE UNITED STATES.

YES, EVEN WATERBOARDING HAS BEEN INDISPENSABLE TO OUR SUCCESS!

THE CIA PROVIDED INFORMATION TO THE CIA OFFICE OF INSPECTOR GENERAL THAT "EITS [INCLUDING THE WATERBOARD] HAVE BEEN INDISPENSABLE TO OUR SUCCESSES," AND STATED THAT THE CIA OIG REVIEW SHOULD HAVE CONCLUDED "THAT OUR EFFORTS HAVE THWARTED ATTACKS AND SAVED LIVES."

CIA REPRESENTATIONS, HOWEVER, OMIT SIGNIFICANT INFORMATION GAINED PRIOR TO ANY REPORTING FROM DETAINEES CONCERNING THE PARACHA FAMILY'S CONNECTIONS TO AL-QA'IDA AND INTERNATIONAL TERRORISM.

THERE IS SO MUCH INFORMATION THAT THE CIA KNEW ABOUT THE PARACHAS PRIOR TO THE USE OF EITS ON KSM. AN ADDRESS ASSOCIATED WITH SAIFULLAH PARACHA'S BUSINESS AS WELL AS A PHONE NUMBER WAS FOUND IN DOCUMENTS SEIZED ON MARCH 28, 2002, IN A RAID AGAINST AL-QA'IDA TARGETS.

AND WHAT DO WE HAVE HERE?

DON'T ANYONE GET EXCITED, THIS IS JUST A ROUTINE INVESTIGATION.

IN APRIL 2002, THE FBI OPENED AN INVESTIGATION ON ANOTHER NEW YORK-BASED BUSINESS ASSOCIATED WITH SAIFULLAH PARACHA AND ACQUIRED ADDITIONAL INFORMATION ON THE BUSINESS AND THE PARACHAS.

THEY MAY WONDER . . . BUT I THINK WE KNOW!

SAIFULLAH PARACHA'S NAME WAS PROVIDED TO PAKISTANI OFFICIALS BY THE CIA IN DECEMBER 2002. THE CIA WROTE, "INFORMATION BELOW LEADS US TO BELIEVE THAT THE FOLLOWING INDIVIDUAL AND PHONE NUMBERS MAY HAVE A CONNECTION TO AL-QA'IDA AND INTERNATIONAL TERRORISM."

THE REQUEST INCLUDED THREE PHONE NUMBERS, ONE OF WHICH WAS ASSOCIATED WITH SAIFULLAH PARACHA'S KARACHI-BASED COMPANY INTERNATIONAL MERCHANDISE PVT. LTD.

DUELING DECLARATIONS

I WOULD DO IT AGAIN.

TORTURE IS WHAT THE AL-QA'IDA TERRORISTS DID TO 3,000 AMERICANS ON 9/11. THERE IS NO COMPARISON BETWEEN THAT AND WHAT WE DID WITH RESPECT TO ENHANCED INTERROGATION.

VICE PRESIDENT DICK CHENEY

FORMER CIA DIRECTOR JOHN O. BRENNAN

"[THE INTERROGATION METHODS] LED US ASTRAY FROM OUR IDEALS AS A NATION . . . TACTICS SUCH AS WATERBOARDING WERE NOT IN KEEPING WITH OUR VALUES AS A NATION."

THE NEW YORK TIMES

"WE HAVE NOT ALWAYS AGREED WITH SENATOR DIANNE FEINSTEIN ON NATIONAL SECURITY ISSUES LIKE WIRETAPPING, BUT THE CALIFORNIA DEMOCRAT WHO HEADS THE SENATE INTELLIGENCE COMMITTEE HAS DISPLAYED COMMITMENT AND COURAGE IN THE INVESTIGATION OF THE ILLEGAL DETENTION, ABUSE, AND TORTURE OF PRISONERS OF THE CENTRAL INTELLIGENCE AGENCY."

FINANCIAL DOCUMENTS SEIZED ON SEPTEMBER 11, 2002, IDENTIFIED AN E-MAIL ADDRESS ATTRIBUTED TO INTERNATIONAL MERCHANDISE PVT LTD WITH THE SAME CONTACT--SAIFULLAH PARACHA. THE CIA INFORMED THE FBI, THE NSA, AND THE DEPARTMENT OF THE TREASURY THAT THEY SUSPECTED SAIFULLAH PARACHA AS WELL AS INTERNATIONAL MERCHANDISE PVT LTD WERE ENGAGED IN TERRORIST FINANCING ACTIVITIES. SPECIFICALLY FOR AL-QA'IDA.

TAKE A LOOK AT THIS!

LOOK AT THAT! FARIS IS GOING INTO THE INTERNATIONAL MERCHANDISING BUILDING!

I'D SAY MUCH LESS OF A BEARD AND, YES, MORE OF A MOUSTACHE.

ARRGHH!

FBI INVESTIGATIVE ACTIVITY OF TERROR-ISM SUSPECT IYMAN FARIS FOUND THAT FARIS WAS LINKED TO PARACHA IMPORTS VIA HIS OHIO-BASED HOUSEMATES.

AND, FINALLY, MAJID KHAN, WHO WAS IN FOREIGN GOVERNMENT CUSTODY, PRO-VIDED REPORTING THAT "UZHAIR" RAN THE NEW YORK BRANCH OF HIS FATHER'S KARACHI-BASED BUSINESS. UZHAIR WAS ASSISTING KHAN AND AMMAR AL-BALUCHI IN THEIR EFFORTS TO RESETTLE KHAN IN THE UNITED STATES FOR TERRORISM-RELATED PURPOSES. KHAN PROVIDED A DETAILED PHYSICAL DESCRIPTION OF BOTH UZHAIR AND SAIFULLAH.

KSM WAS CAPTURED ON MARCH 1, 2003, AND RENDERED INTO CIA CUSTODY AND IMMEDIATELY SUB-JECTED TO EITS. A CIA REPORT FROM MARCH 24, 2003, STATES THAT DURING THAT AFTERNOON, KSM HAD BEEN SUBJECTED TO ENHANCED TECHNIQUES, INCLUDING THE WATERBOARD, FOR FAILING TO PROVIDE INFORMATION ON OPERATIONS IN THE UNITED STATES AND FOR HAVING "LIED ABOUT POISON AND BIOLOG-ICAL WARFARE PROGRAMS."

THAT EVENING, KSM'S INTERROGATORS RECEIVED INFORMATION PROVIDED BY MAJID KHAN, WHO WAS IN FOREIGN GOVERNMENT CUSTODY AND BEING INTERVIEWED BY FBI AGENTS AND FOREIGN GOVERNMENT OFFICERS. CIA CABLES DESCRIBE KSM AS BEING "BOXED IN" BY THIS REPORTING AND THEN PROVIDING A GREAT DEAL OF INFORMATION.

WHEN CONFRONTED WITH DETAILS OF HIS ROLE IN THE PLOT TO SMUGGLE EXPLOSIVES INTO THE UNITED STATES, AS PROVIDED BY KHAN, KSM CLAIMED THAT PARACHA AGREED TO USE HIS TEXTILE BUSINESS TO SMUGGLE EXPLOSIVES INTO THE UNITED STATES AND WAS ARRANGING THE DETAILS WITH AMMAR AL-BALUCHI AND KHAN AT THE TIME OF KSM'S CAPTURE.

MAJID KHAN SAID WHAT?

AND, YES, I WAS CLOSE TO UZHAIR'S FATHER AND DID HELP HIM FIND SAFE HOUSES IN KARACHI.

ON JULY 5, 2003, SAIFULLAH PARACHA WAS DETAINED IN AN OPERATION ORCHESTRATED BY THE FBI. SHORTLY THEREAFTER, SAIFULLAH PARACHA WAS RENDERED TO U.S. MILITARY CUSTODY AT BAGRAM AIR BASE.

YES . . . THE MAN IS NO LIAR.

THE CIA MADE REPEATED CLAIMS THAT THE USE OF EITS RESULTED IN "KEY INTELLIGENCE" FROM ABU ZUBAYDAH AND KSM ON AN OPERATIVE NAMED JAFFAR AL-TAYYAR, LATER IDENTIFIED AS ADNAN EL-SHUKRIJU-MAH. THESE REPRESENTATIONS, THEY STATED, RESULTED IN AN FBI INVESTI-GATION THAT PROMPTED AL-TAYYAR TO FLEE THE COUNTRY.

THESE REPRESENTATIONS WERE INAC-CURATE. KSM WAS CAPTURED ON MARCH 1, 2003. AL-TAYYAR DEPARTED THE UNITED STATES ALMOST TWO YEARS EARLIER IN MAY 2001!

CIA REPRESENTATIONS ALSO OMIT-TED KEY FACTS, INCLUDING THAT THE INTELLIGENCE COMMUNITY WAS INTERESTED IN THE FLORIDA-BASED EL-SHUKRIJUMAH PRIOR TO THE DETENTION OF ZUBAYDAH, THE CIA'S FIRST DETAINEE. HE PROVIDED A DE-SCRIPTION AND INFORMATION ON A KSM ASSOCIATE NAMED AL-TAYYAR TO FBI SPECIAL AGENTS IN MAY 2002, PRIOR TO HIS BEING SUBJECTED TO THE CIA'S ENHANCED TECHNIQUES.

OTHER KEY FACTS THAT WERE OMITTED INCLUDE THAT CIA PERSONNEL DISTRUSTED KSM'S REPORTING ON AL-TAYYAR, CLAIMING HE FABRICATED INFOR-MATION; OTHER CIA DETAINEES' REPORTING DIFFERED FROM KSM'S IN SIGNIFICANT WAYS; AND CIA RECORDS INDICATE THAT JOSÉ PADILLA, QUESTIONED BY THE FBI WHILE IN MILITARY CUSTODY, NOT KSM, IDENTIFIED AL-TAYYAR'S TRUE NAME AS EL-SHUKRIJUMAH.

ALRIGHT, STOP! I'LL GIVE YOU ANOTHER NAME . . . SALEH AL-MARRI.

I KNEW IT WOULD WORK.

THE CIA'S EVALUATION AND DESCRIPTION OF ITS DETENTION AND INTERROGATION PROGRAM DIDN'T CHANGE OVER THE YEARS. ON MARCH 2, 2005, THEY CLAIMED IT "HAS ENABLED THE CIA TO DISRUPT TERRORIST PLOTS, CAPTURE ADDITIONAL TERRORISTS, AND COLLECT A HIGH VOLUME OF CRITICAL INTELLIGENCE ON AL-QA'IDA."

ADNAN?

HE'S BEEN IN PAKISTAN FOR ALMOST A YEAR!

THE CIA ALSO REPRESENTED THAT PRIOR TO REPORTING FROM KSM, THE CIA POSSESSED "NO CONCRETE INFORMATION" ON AL-MARRI. THIS INFORMATION IS INCORRECT. CIA RECORDS INDICATE THEY POSSESSED SIGNIFICANT INFOR- MATION ON THE MAN. HE HAD BEEN ARRESTED AFTER MAKING ATTEMPTS TO CONTACT A TELE- PHONE NUMBER ASSOCIATED WITH AN AL-QA'IDA MEMBER, HE HAD SUSPICIOUS INFORMATION ON HIS COMPUTER, AND HIS BROTHER HAD GONE TO AFGHANISTAN IN 2001 TO JOIN IN JIHAD AGAINST THE UNITED STATES.

CIA REPRESENTATIONS THAT JAFFAR AL-TAYYAR FLED THE UNITED STATES IN 2003 IN RESPONSE TO AN INVESTIGATION PROMPTED BY REPORTING FROM KSM WERE INCONSISTENT WITH CIA RECORDS AT THE TIME. THESE RECORDS REPORTED THAT HE HAD ALREADY RELOCATED TO PAKISTAN.

IN MARCH 2003, WHEN JOSÉ PADILLA IDEN- TIFIED AL-TAYYAR AS ADNAN AL-SHUKRIJUMAH, HE SAID HE HAD LAST SEEN HIM AT A KSM SAFE HOUSE IN KARACHI, PAKISTAN, IN MARCH 2002.

THE CIA REPRESENTED THAT AS A RESULT OF THE LAWFUL USE OF EITS, KSM "PROVIDED INFORMATION THAT HELPED LEAD TO THE ARREST OF TERRORISTS . . . INCLUDING SALEH AL-MARRI, A SLEEPER OPERATIVE IN NEW YORK."

THIS INFORMATION WAS INACCURATE. KSM WAS CAPTURED ON MARCH 1, 2003. SALEH AL-MARRI WAS ARRESTED IN DECEMBER 2001.

AND WHAT DO I SEE HERE ON YOUR COMPUTER, MR. AL-MARRI?

OVER SEVERAL YEARS, THE CIA REPRESENTED TO POLI-
CYMAKERS THAT "KEY INTELLIGENCE" WAS OBTAINED
FROM THE USE OF EITS, SUCH AS REVEALING THAT SHKAI,
PAKISTAN, WAS A "MAJOR AL-QA'IDA HUB IN THE TRIBAL
AREAS" THAT RESULTED IN "TACTICAL INTELLIGENCE."
THESE REPRESENTATIONS WERE BASED ON CIA EXPERI-
ENCE WITH ONE DETAINEE, HASSAN GHUL.

WHY ARE YOU DOING THIS TO ME?

WHY ARE YOU NOT TELLING US WHAT WE ASK YOU?

AND, OF COURSE, I WOULD POINT OUT THE IMPORTANCE OF SHKAI IN PAKISTAN!

BUT ACCORDING TO OTHER CIA RECORDS, GHUL WAS CAPTURED BY FOREIGN AUTHORITIES IN IRAQ IN JANUARY 2004, GIVEN TO THE CIA LATER THAT MONTH, AND PROVIDED INFORMATION FOR AT LEAST 21 INTELLIGENCE REPORTS, INCLUDING THE IMPORTANCE OF SHKAI, *WITHOUT* THE USE OF EITS.

HE HAD BEEN PLACED IN A CELL, GIVEN ADEQUATE CLOTHING, BEDDING, WATER, AND A WASTE BUCKET. HIS REPORTS INCLUDED INFORMATION ON THE LOCATION, MOVEMENTS, OPERATIONAL SECURITY, AND TRAINING OF SENIOR AL-QA'IDA LEADERS LIVING IN SHKAI AS WELL AS THE VISITS OF LEADERS AND OPERATIVES TO THE AREA. HE ALSO INCLUDED DETAILS OF VARIOUS GROUPS OPERATING IN THE AREA AND THE CONFLICTS AMONG THEM.

ACCORDING TO GHUL'S REPORTS, AS OF
DECEMBER 2003, APPROXIMATELY 60
ARAB MALES AND BETWEEN 150 AND 200
TURKIC/UZBEK MALES WERE LIVING IN
SHKAI, ALONG WITH A "SIGNIFICANT POPULA-
TION" OF BALUCHIS WHO ASSISTED THE
ARABS AND UZBEKS.

YES, ALL THIS WITHOUT THE USE OF A
SINGLE EIT.

I BELIEVE I WILL BE COMFORTABLE HERE.

I'LL GIVE YOU WHATEVER TELEPHONE NUMBERS I KNOW.

AFTER TWO DAYS AT THIS CIA DETENTION CENTER, HASSAN GHUL WAS TRANSFERRED TO **DETENTION SITE BLACK.** THERE HE WAS IMMEDIATELY AND FOR THE FIRST TIME SUBJECTED TO EITS! HE WAS "SHAVED AND BARBERED, STRIPPED, AND PLACED IN THE STANDING POSITION."

WHERE HE TOLD THEM *NOTHING!*

GHUL'S REPORTING ON SHKAI PRIOR TO THE USE OF EITS WAS COMPILED BY THE CIA AND SENT TO THE PAKISTANI GOVERNMENT. THE CIA LATER REPLIED THAT HIS INFORMATION "MOVED SHKAI TO THE FOREFRONT" AND THAT THEY WERE REVISITING THE SITUATION.

A LATER RETURN CABLE HIGHLY PRAISED GHUL AND HE WAS LATER RELEASED.

SHORTLY AFTER THE RAID ON THE USAMA BIN LADEN COMPOUND ON MAY 1, 2011, RESULTING IN BIN LADEN'S DEATH, CIA OFFICIALS CLAIMED THE USE OF EITS AS PART OF THE STORY.

THIS WAS INACCURATE AND INCONGRUENT WITH CIA RECORDS.

THE RECORDS INDICATE THAT THE CIA HAD EXTENSIVE REPORTING ON ABU AHMED AL-KUWAITI, THE BIN LADEN FACILITATOR ALSO KILLED IN THE RAID, WHOSE IDENTIFICATION AND TRACKING LED TO THE IDENTIFICATION OF UBL'S COMPOUND. BUT ALL THAT WAS PRIOR TO AND INDEPENDENT OF INFORMATION FROM CIA DETAINEES.

THE CIA DID NOT RECEIVE ANY INFOR-
MATION FROM CIA DETAINEES ON ABU
AHMED AL-KUWAITI UNTIL 2003. NONE-
THELESS, BY THE END OF 2002, THEY
WERE ACTIVELY TARGETING THE MAN AND
HAD COLLECTED SIGNIFICANT REPORTING
ON HIS CLOSE LINKS TO USAMA BIN LADEN.

AND THOSE TWO MEN,
GENTLEMEN, ARE OUR
BIGGEST CONCERNS!

FORGET THOSE WOMEN
I GOT YOU, DO I HAVE A
NUMBER FOR YOU!

CIA RECORDS INDICATE THAT PRIOR TO
RECEIVING ANY INFORMATION FROM DETAIN-
EES, AS EARLY AS JANUARY 1, 2002, A PHONE
NUMBER ASSOCIATED WITH AL-KUWAITI WAS IN
THEIR POSSESSION. IN MARCH 2002, THE
NUMBER WAS FOUND IN ABU ZUBAYDAH'S
ADDRESS BOOK. AND IN APRIL 2002, THAT
SAME NUMBER WAS FOUND TO BE IN CON-
TACT WITH BIN LADEN FAMILY MEMBERS. ALL
THIS PRIOR TO ANY REPORTING FROM CIA
DETAINEES.

I THINK WE'RE BEGINNING
TO GET A PICTURE OF WHO
THEY ARE!

IN JULY 2002, THE CIA OBTAINED AN E-MAIL
ADDRESS ASSOCIATED WITH AL-KUWAITI, AND BY
AUGUST 24 THEY WERE TRACKING HIS E-MAIL
ACTIVITY. A DETAINEE IN A FOREIGN GOVERNMENT'S
CUSTODY REPORTED THAT AL-KUWAITI SHARED AN
E-MAIL ADDRESS WITH AMMAR AL-BALUCHI AND
THAT AL-KUWAITI WAS "COORDINATING MARTYRDOM
OPERATIONS."

ALL THIS INFORMATION WAS ACQUIRED PRIOR TO
REPORTS ON THE SUBJECT FROM CIA DETAINEES.

ON JUNE 10, 2002, THE CIA RECEIVED
REPORTING FROM A FOREIGN-HELD DE-
TAINEE THAT AL-KUWAITI WAS ENGAGED IN
ATTACK PLANNING WITH KSM. ON JUNE 25,
ANOTHER FOREIGN-HELD DETAINEE COR-
ROBORATED THE STORY THAT AL-KUWAITI
WORKED ON "SECRET OPERATIONS" WITH
KSM PRIOR TO THE 9/11 ATTACKS.

ON OCTOBER 20, 2002, THE CIA
RECEIVED FURTHER INFORMATION CON-
CERNING HASSAN GHUL'S RECEIPT OF
INSTRUCTIONS FROM A CLOSE ASSOCIATE
OF KSM. ALL PRIOR TO ANY REPORTING ON
AL-KUWAITI FROM CIA DETAINEES.

NOW TELL ME AGAIN HIS
APPROXIMATE AGE AND THE
COLOR OF HIS HAIR.

IT'S IN
A CODE,
BUT I
THINK
I'VE GOT
IT!

IN SEPTEMBER 2001, THE CIA RECEIVED
REPORTING ON AL-KUWAITI'S FAMILY THAT THE
CIA WOULD LATER CITE AS PIVOTAL IN IDENTI-
FYING HIS TRUE NAME. FROM JANUARY
THROUGH OCTOBER 2002, THE CIA RECEIVED
SIGNIFICANT CORROBORATION REPORTING ON
HIS AGE, PHYSICAL APPEARANCE, AND FAMILY
FROM DETAINEES HELD IN FOREIGN CUSTODY
OR CUSTODY OF THE U.S. MILITARY. ALL THIS
INFORMATION WAS ACQUIRED PRIOR TO ANY
REPORTING FROM CIA DETAINEES.

LOOK AT THIS AL-KUWAITI PHONE NUMBER! IT ALSO IS TIED TO A BIN LADEN!

AS EARLY AS APRIL 2002, THE CIA LINKED A PHONE NUMBER ASSOCIATED WITH AL-KUWAITI WITH USAMA BIN LADEN'S FAMILY, SPECIFICALLY SA'AD BIN LADEN. ON JUNE 5, 2002, THE CIA RECEIVED REPORTING FROM A FOREIGN-HELD DETAINEE, FORMER BIN LADEN CARETAKER RIDHA AL-NAJJAR, THAT "ABU AHMED" WAS ONE OF THREE AL-QA'IDA-ASSOCIATED INDIVIDUALS--INCLUDING SA'AD BIN LADEN AND KSM--TO VISIT USAMA.

I'M CARRYING A MESSAGE FROM YOU KNOW WHO.

ON JUNE 25, 2002, THE CIA RECEIVED REPORTING FROM ANOTHER FOREIGN-HELD DETAINEE, RIYADH THE FACILITATOR, THAT AL-KUWAITI MAY HAVE BEEN A BIN LADEN COURIER.

HE BELIEVED AL-KUWAITI "WAS ACTIVELY WORKING IN SECRET LOCATIONS IN KARACHI, BUT TRAVELED FREQUENTLY" TO MEET UBL. MONTHS EARLIER, THE CIA INDICATED THAT ABU AHMED AL-KUWAITI AND RIYADH WERE IN CONTACT WITH EACH OTHER.

AL-KUWAITI, BESIDES THE NEWS YOU BRING ME, YOU BRING ME SMILES AND LAUGHS!

AND IN AUGUST 2002, STILL ANOTHER FOREIGN-HELD DETAINEE WITH KNOWN LINKS TO AL-KUWAITI REPORTED THAT AL-KUWAITI "WAS ONE OF THE FEW CLOSE ASSOCIATES" OF UBL.

ALL OF THIS INFORMATION WAS ACQUIRED IN 2002, PRIOR TO ANY REPORTING ON AL-KUWAITI FROM CIA DETAINEES.

YES, THAT IS ABU AHMED!

ON MAY 2, 2011, THE CIA INFORMED THE SSCI THAT "ABU AHMED HAD TOTALLY DROPPED OFF OUR RADAR IN ABOUT 2002-2003 . . . AFTER SEVERAL DETAINEES IN OUR CUSTODY HAD HIGHLIGHTED HIM AS A KEY FACILITATOR."

THIS, OF COURSE, IS NOT CONGRUENT WITH CIA RECORDS. NO CIA DETAINEE PROVIDED INFORMATION ON THE MAN UNTIL THE SPRING OF 2003.

I AM SURE YOU WILL BE SAFE HERE, ABU!

BIN LADEN TODAY, MAYBE ISIS TOMORROW!

SOON AFTER THE RAID ON THE BIN LADEN COMPOUND ON MAY 1, 2011, CIA OFFICIALS DESCRIBED THE ROLE OF THE CIA'S INTERROGATION PROGRAM IN THE OPERATION AND, IN SOME CASES, CONNECTED THE PROGRAM TO THE OPERATION'S SUCCESS.

THE VAST MAJORITY OF DOCUMENTS, STATEMENTS, AND TESTIMONY PRESENTED HIGHLIGHTING THE SUPPOSED USE OF THIS PROGRAM WAS INACCURATE AND INCONGRUENT WITH CIA RECORDS.

GENTLEMEN, WE ARE READY . . .

AL-KUWAITI? I NEVER EVEN HEARD THAT NAME BEFORE!

CIA RECORDS INDICATE THAT THE CIA HAD EXPANSIVE REPORTING ON AL-KUWAITI, THE FACILITATOR WHOSE IDENTIFICATION AND TRACKING LED TO THE LOCATION OF BIN LADEN'S COMPOUND PRIOR TO AND INDEPENDENT OF INFORMATION FROM CIA DETAINEES.

AND THE MOST ACCURATE INFORMATION ON AL-KUWAITI WAS OBTAINED FROM A CIA DETAINEE NOT YET SUBJECTED TO EITS.

CIA DETAINEES SUBJECTED TO EITS WITHHELD AND FABRICATED INFORMATION ABOUT AL-KUWAITI.

WITHIN A DAY OF THE BIN LADEN OPER-ATION, THE CIA BEGAN PREPARING CLASSIFIED BRIEFINGS TO CONGRESS ON THE OVERALL OPERATION AND INTELLIGENCE THAT LED TO THE RAID AND TO BIN LADEN'S DEATH. ON MAY 2, 2011, CIA OFFICIALS, INCLUDING DEP-UTY DIRECTOR MICHAEL MORELL, BRIEFED THE SSCI. ON MAY 4, 2011, CIA DIRECTOR LEON PANETTA AND OTHER CIA OFFICIALS BRIEFED BOTH THE SSCI AND THE SENATE ARMED SER-VICE COMMITTEE.

THE TESTIMONIES CONTAINED SIGNIF-ICANT INACCURACIES.

IN THE MAY 2 BRIEFING, THE CIA INFORMED THE SSCI . . .

THERE REMAINED ONE PRIMARY LINE OF INVESTIGATION THAT WAS PROVING MOST DIFFICULT TO RUN TO GROUND . . . THE CASE OF ABU AHMED AL-KUWAITI.

HE HAD TOTALLY DROPPED OFF OUR RADAR IN ABOUT 2002-2003 . . . AFTER SEVERAL DETAINEES IN OUR CUSTODY HAD HIGHLIGHTED HIM AS A KEY FACILITATOR FOR BIN LADEN.

UH, EXCUSE ME, SIR, BUT I THINK YOU HAVE THAT WRONG.

THAT INFORMATION IS NOT FULLY CONGRUENT WITH CIA RECORDS. THE CIA WAS TARGETING AL-KUWAITI PRIOR TO ANY REPORTING FROM CIA DETAINEES. HE WAS IDENTIFIED AS EARLY AS 2002 AS AN AL-QA'IDA MEMBER ENGAGED IN OPERATIONAL PLANNING WHO TRAVELED OFTEN TO SEE USAMA BIN LADEN . . .

NO CIA DETAINEE PROVIDED REPORTING ON HIM IN 2002, AND THE MOST ACCURATE INTELLIGENCE WAS COLLECTED OUTSIDE THE DETEN-TION AND INTERROGATION PROGRAM. AND THAT WAS NOT FROM DETAINEES IN CIA CUSTODY BUT FROM OTHER INTELLIGENCE SOURCES.

NO, LET'S NOT BOTHER UBL WITH THIS NONSENSE.

ON MAY 2, 2011, CIA DIRECTOR LEON PANETTA PROVIDED THE FOLLOWING STATEMENT TO THE SSCI AND THE SENATE ARMED SERVICES COMMITTEE . . .

WE THINK THERE WERE ABOUT 12 DETAINEES THAT WERE INTERVIEWED, AND ABOUT THREE OF THEM WERE PROBABLY SUBJECTED TO THE WATERBOARDING PROCESS . . .

WE HAD INFORMATION THAT CAME FROM A NUMBER OF DIRECTIONS IN ORDER TO PIECE THIS TOGETHER. BUT CLEARLY THE TIP-OFF ON THE COURIERS WERE FROM THESE INTERVIEWS.

THE DETAINEES IN THE POST-9/11 PERIOD FLAGGED FOR US THAT THERE WERE INDIVIDUALS THAT PROVIDED DIRECT SUPPORT TO BIN LADEN . . . AND ONE OF THOSE IDENTIFIED WAS A COURIER WHO HAD THE NICKNAME ABU AHMED AL-KUWAITI.

FOR THE STATEMENT TO BE ACCURATE IT CAN ONLY BE A REFERENCE TO DETAIN-EES IN *FOREIGN GOVERNMENT CUSTODY!*

AT THE MAY 4, 2011, BRIEFING, A SENA-TOR ASKED CIA DIRECTOR PANETTA, "OF THE PEOPLE THAT YOU TALKED ABOUT AS DETAINEES THAT WERE INTERROGATED, WHICH OF THOSE WERE WATERBOARDED AND DID THEY PROVIDE UNIQUE INTELLI-GENCE IN ORDER TO MAKE THIS WHOLE MISSION POSSIBLE?"

THE SO-CALLED TIP-OFF DID NOT COME FROM THE INTERROGATION OF CIA DETAINEES AND WAS OBTAINED PRIOR TO ANY CIA DETAINEE REPORTING.

OH YES, WE GOT IT FROM ABU ZUBAYDAH AND RIYADH THE FACILITATOR IN 2002.

IN A LATER BRIEFING, AN UNSPECIFIED CIA OFFICER TESTIFIED ABOUT THE CIA'S SUPPOSED FIRST KNOWLEDGE OF AL-KUWAITI . . .

THIS IS INACCURATE. THE INITIAL LEAD ON AL-KUWAITI WAS COLLECTED BY THE CIA FROM OTHER INTELLIGENCE SOURCES, INCLUDING DETAINEES IN FOREIGN GOVERNMENT CUSTODY.

NO, I DO NOT MIND TALKING ABOUT HIM.

FOR CERTAIN, AL-KUWAITI IS CLOSE TO BIN LADEN.

THE CIA DETAINEE WHO PROVIDED THE MOST ACCURATE "TIER 1" INFORMATION LINKING AL-KUWAITI TO BIN LADEN WAS HASSAN GHUL PRIOR TO HIS BEING SUBJECTED TO EITS.

THE CIA DISSEMINATED 21 INTELLIGENCE REPORTS BASED ON GHUL'S REPORTING. HE "OPENED UP RIGHT AWAY AND WAS COOPERATIVE FROM THE OUTSET," A CIA OFFICER TOLD THE OIG.

AND **THIS** IS MY REWARD?

BUT THE DAY AFTER HE PROVIDED HIS STATEMENTS, GHUL WAS TRANSFERRED TO A NEW SITE WHERE HE WAS "SHAVED AND BARBERED, STRIPPED AND PLACED IN THE STANDING POSITION AGAINST THE WALL" FOR 40 MINUTES.

INTERROGATORS IMMEDIATELY REQUESTED PERMISSION TO USE EITS DURING THESE 40 MINUTES. HE DID **NOT** PROVIDE ANY NEW INFORMATION, DID NOT SHOW FEAR, AND WAS "SOMEWHAT ARROGANT AND SELF-IMPORTANT."

CIA HEADQUARTERS APPROVED THE REQUEST TO USE EITS THE SAME DAY, STATING THAT EITS WOULD "INCREASE BASE'S CAPABILITY TO COLLECT CRITICAL AND RELIABLE THREAT INFORMATION IN A TIMELY MANNER."

DURING AND AFTER THE USE OF THE TECHNIQUES, GHUL PROVIDED NO OTHER SUBSTANTIAL INFORMATION ON AL-KUWAITI AND HE WAS LATER RELEASED.

WHAT ARE YOU GOING TO DO WITH ME NOW?

SO WHY ARE WE DOING THIS?

DESPITE CIA CLAIMS OF GREAT SUCCESS WITH THEIR TECHNIQUES, THEY INTERNALLY NOTED THAT REPORTINGS FROM CIA DETAINEES, SPECIFICALLY THOSE SUBJECTED TO THESE TECHNIQUES, WAS INSUFFICIENT, FABRICATED, AND/OR UNRELIABLE.

A SIMILAR NOTE CAME ON SEPTEMBER 1, 2005, WHEN A REPORT ON THE SEARCH FOR BIN LADEN STATED, "DETAINEES PROVIDE FEW ACTIONABLE LEADS, AND WE HAVE TO CONSIDER THE POSSIBILITY THAT THEY ARE CREATING FICTITIOUS CHARACTERS TO DISTRACT US OR TO ABSOLVE THEMSELVES."

YES, I WILL GIVE YOU HIS NAME. IT IS ABOU BEN ADAM.

AND ON MAY 20, 2007, A CIA TARGETING STUDY FOR AL-KUWAITI REPORTED THAT KSM "DESCRIBED ABU AHMED AS A RELATIVELY MINOR FIGURE AND ABU FARAJ AL-LIBI DENIED ALL KNOWLEDGE OF ABU AHMED. STATION ASSESSES THAT KSM AND ABU FARAJ'S REPORTING IS NOT CREDIBLE."

OVERVIEW OF CIA REPRESENTATIONS TO THE MEDIA WHILE PROGRAM WAS CLASSIFIED

I WILL BE AS COMPLETE AS I CAN WITH YOU, BUT WE NEVER CAN BE QUOTED OR YOUR SOURCE REVEALED.

UNDERSTOOD.

SEEKING TO SHAPE PRESS REPORTING ON THE CIA'S DETENTION AND INTERROGATION PROGRAM, THE CIA OFFICE OF PUBLIC AFFAIRS PROVIDED BACKGROUND INFORMATION ON THE PROGRAM TO JOURNALISTS FOR BOOKS, ARTICLES, AND BROADCASTS, EVEN WHEN THE PROGRAM WAS CLASSIFIED.

WHEN JOURNALISTS WHO HAD BEEN PROVIDED THIS BACKGROUND MATERIAL PUBLISHED CLASSIFIED INFORMATION, THE CIA DID NOT, AS A MATTER OF POLICY, SUBMIT CRIME REPORTS.

THE BOOK CONTAINED NO FIRST-TIME DISCLOSURES.

AND OUR OFFICE OF PUBLIC AFFAIRS PROVIDED ASSISTANCE TO MR. KESSLER.

THE CIA AT WAR

INSIDE THE SECRET CAMPAIGN AGAINST TERROR

RONALD KESSLER

THOUGH CIA OFFICERS AND THE HOUSE PERMANENT SELECT COMMITTEE ON INTELLIGENCE RAISED CONCERNS, THE CIA NEVER OPENED AN INVESTIGATION RELATED TO RONALD KESSLER'S BOOK, *THE CIA AT WAR*, OR JEHL'S *NEW YORK TIMES* ARTICLE, DESPITE THE INCLUSION OF CLASSIFIED INFORMATION, BECAUSE "PART OF THIS ARTICLE WAS BASED ON 'BACKGROUND' PROVIDED BY OPA. THAT, ESSENTIALLY, NEGATES ANY USE IN MAKING AN UNAUTHORIZED DISCLOSURE [REPORT]."

BOTH THE BOOK AND THE ARTICLE INCLUDE INACCURATE CLAIMS ABOUT THE EFFECTIVENESS OF THE INTERROGATION PROGRAM THAT WERE CONSISTENT WITH CIA REPRESENTATIONS AT THE TIME.

ON JUNE 24, 2005, DATELINE NBC AIRED A PROGRAM THAT INCLUDED ON-THE-RECORD QUOTES OF CIA DIRECTOR PORTER GOSS AND DEPUTY CTC DIRECTOR PHILIP MUDD AND INCLUDED SUCH DECLARATIONS AS . . .

"AL-QA'IDA LEADERS SUDDENLY FOUND THEMSELVES BUNDLED INTO A CIA GULFSTREAM V OR BOEING 737 JET HEADED FOR LONG MONTHS OF INTERROGATION."

"THE CAPTURE OF RAMZI BIN AL-SHIBH LED TO THE CAPTURE OF KSM AND KHALLAD BIN ATTASH."

ALL THIS WAS INACCURATE. THERE ARE NO CIA RECORDS SHOWING THERE WAS ANY INVESTIGATION OR CRIME REPORTS SUBMITTED IN CONNECTION WITH THIS PROGRAM AND ITS REPORTING.

ON SEPTEMBER 7, 2006, THE DAY AFTER PRESIDENT BUSH PUBLICLY ACKNOWLEDGED THE DETENTION AND INTERROGATION PROGRAM, DAVID JOHNSTON OF THE *NEW YORK TIMES* CALLED THE CIA WITH A PROPOSED NEWS STORY ABOUT THE INTERROGATION OF ABU ZUBAYDAH. THE CIA DIRECTOR OF PUBLIC AFFAIRS DESCRIBED JOHNSTON'S PROPOSED STORY AS . . .

BULLSHIT!

BIASED TOWARD THE FBI! AND *WE NEED TO PUSH BACK!*

ABU ZUBAYDAH COOPERATED WITH FBI INTERVIEWERS.

OFFICIAL MORE CLOSELY ALLIED WITH LAW ENFORCEMENT

ON SEPTEMBER 10, 2006, JOHNSTON'S ARTICLE APPEARED. TITLED "AT A SECRET INTERROGATION, DISPUTE FLARED OVER TACTICS," IT DESCRIBED "SHARPLY CONTRASTING ACCOUNTS" OF THE INTERROGATION OF ZUBAYDAH.

ZUBAYDAH WAS LYING AND THINGS WERE GOING NOWHERE. BUT TOUGHER TACTICS BEGAN TO PROVIDE INFORMATION ON KEY AL-QA'IDA OPERATIONS.

OFFICIAL CLOSELY TIED TO INTELLIGENCE AGENCIES

HE GIVES UNDUE CREDIT TO THE FBI FOR CIA ACCOMPLISHMENTS!

IF WE ARE GOING TO DO THIS, THE CIA SHOULD PROVIDE INFORMATION THAT WOULD UNDERCUT THE FBI.

IN EARLY 2007, THE CIA COOPERATED WITH RONALD KESSLER ON ANOTHER BOOK. ACCORDING TO CIA RECORDS, THE PURPOSE WAS TO "PUSH BACK" ON HIS PROPOSED ACCOUNTS OF INTELLIGENCE RELATED TO THE 9/11 ATTACKS AND THE INTERROGATION OF ZUBAYDAH. CIA AGENTS APPLAUDING THE PURPOSE ADDED . . .

WHO STATED THAT THEY COULD HAVE GOTTEN EVERYTHING ANYWAY?

HE WAS VASTLY OVERSTATING THE FBI'S ROLE IN THWARTING TERRORISM!

AND, FRANKLY, GIVING OTHER USG AGENCIES SHORT SHRIFT!

THE DRAFT ALSO DIDN'T REFLECT THE ENORMOUSLY VALUABLE INTELLIGENCE THE UNITED STATES GLEANED FROM THE CIA'S INTERROGATION PROGRAM!

AFTER RONALD KESSLER PROVIDED A DRAFT OF HIS BOOK TO THE CIA AND MET WITH THEIR OFFICERS, CIA DIRECTOR OF PUBLIC AFFAIRS MARK MANSFIELD DESCRIBED WHAT HE SAW AS THE NARRATIVE'S PROBLEMS.

HE ADDED THAT UNNAMED FBI OFFICERS QUESTIONED "OUR METHODS AND CLAIM[ED] THEIR OWN WAY OF ELICITING INFORMATION IS MUCH MORE EFFECTIVE."

ABU ZUBAYDAH WAS SUBJECTED TO "COERCIVE INTERROGATION TECHNIQUES" AFTER HE "STOPPED COOPERATING."

"THE CIA COULD POINT TO A STRING OF SUCCESSES AND DOZENS OF PLOTS THAT WERE ROLLED UP BECAUSE OF COERCIVE INTERROGATION TECHNIQUES."

"WITHOUT WINNING THE WAR BEING WAGED BY THE MEDIA AGAINST OUR OWN GOVERNMENT, WE ARE GOING TO LOSE THE WAR ON TERROR."

IN AN E-MAIL TO MANSFIELD, KESSLER PROVIDED A LIST OF "SUBSTANTIVE CHANGES" HE HAD MADE TO HIS DRAFT FOLLOWING HIS MEETING WITH CIA OFFICIALS.

THE "SUBSTANTIVE CHANGES" KESSLER MADE ALSO INCLUDED THAT MANY MEMBERS OF CONGRESS AND MEMBERS OF THE MEDIA "HAVE MADE CAREERS FOR THEMSELVES BY BELITTLING AND UNDERCUTTING THE EFFORTS OF THE HEROIC MEN AND WOMEN WHO ARE TRYING TO PROTECT US."

AND, FINALLY, KESSLER'S CHANGES INCLUDED: "TOO MANY AMERICANS ARE INTENT ON DEMONIZING THOSE WHO ARE TRYING TO PROTECT US."

REVIEW OF CIA REPRESENTATIONS TO THE DEPARTMENT OF JUSTICE

THE OFFICE OF LEGAL COUNSEL (OLC) IN THE DEPARTMENT OF JUSTICE WROTE SEVERAL MEMORANDA BETWEEN 2002 AND 2007 ON THE LEGALITY OF THE CIA'S DETENTION AND INTERROGATION PROGRAM. MUCH INFORMATION THE CIA PROVIDED WAS INACCURATE. STILL, ON AUGUST 1, 2002, THE OLC GRANTED THAT USE OF THE ENHANCED TECHNIQUES AGAINST ABU ZUBAYDAH WOULD NOT VIOLATE TORTURE PROHIBITIONS.

I'VE BEEN HERE FOR 47 DAYS! WHAT DO THEY WANT FROM ME?

I DON'T KNOW ANYTHING MORE ABOUT AL-QA'IDA!

ABU ZUBAYDAH? I DON'T EVEN KNOW THE NAME. HE COULDN'T BE PART OF THE GROUP.

INFORMATION THE CIA PROVIDED ON ZUBAYDAH WAS ALSO INACCURATE AND UNSUPPORTED BY CIA RECORDS, SUCH AS THAT ZUBAYDAH WAS THE "THIRD OR FOURTH MAN" IN AL-QA'IDA WHEN HE WASN'T EVEN A MEMBER OF THE GROUP.

I DON'T THINK WE'LL NEED ANY MORE THAN FOUR PLANES.

YOU THINK OF YOUR GREATEST MOMENT OF LOVE AND YOU WON'T FEEL A THING!

AND THAT HE "HAS BEEN INVOLVED IN EVERY MAJOR TERRORIST OPERATION CARRIED OUT BY AL-QA'IDA," INCLUDING THE PLANNING OF 9/11. CIA RECORDS DO NOT SUPPORT THESE CLAIMS.

THE CIA ALSO REPRESENTED THAT ZUBAYDAH WAS "WELL-VERSED" IN RESISTANCE TO THE INTERROGATION TECHNIQUES AND "IT IS BELIEVED" HE WROTE THEIR "MANUAL ON RESISTANCE TECHNIQUES." THERE IS NO INFORMATION TO SUPPORT THIS CIA CLAIM.

"THE INTERROGATION TEAM IS CERTAIN," THEY ALSO CLAIMED, THAT ZUBAYDAH WAS WITHHOLDING INFORMATION RELATED TO PLANNED ATTACKS AGAINST THE UNITED STATES.

THERE IS NO CIA RECORD TO SUPPORT THIS CLAIM.

WE'RE ONLY MILES FROM OUR TARGET!

ARE YOU SURE WE'RE SUPPOSED TO DO IT THIS WAY?

JUST FOLLOW MY LEAD.

THE CIA BROADLY INTERPRETED THE AUGUST 1, 2002, MEMO AS ALLOWING GREATER OPERATIONAL LATITUDE DESPITE THE MEMO SPEAKING SPECIFICALLY ABOUT ABU ZUBAYDAH. THE CIA APPLIED IT TO NUMEROUS DETAINEES. AND THOUGH THE OLC DESCRIBED EXACTLY HOW THE TECHNIQUES COULD BE APPLIED, THE CIA APPLIED THEM IN A "QUITE DIFFERENT" MANNER . . .

MOTHER, MOTHER, WHAT ARE YOU DOING HERE? YOU'RE ONLY MAKING IT **WORSE** FOR ME!

AIEEEE!

THE CIA ASSURED THE OLC THAT IT WOULD BE "UNLIKELY" THAT A DETAINEE SUBJECTED TO SLEEP DEPRIVATION WOULD EXPERIENCE HALLUCINATIONS, AND IF HE DID, MEDICAL PER- SONNEL WOULD INTERVENE. HOWEVER, MULTIPLE DETAINEES EXPERIENCED HALLUCINATIONS AND INTERROGATION TEARS AFTER FACING SLEEP DEPRIVATION AND THE TECHNIQUE WAS NOT ALWAYS DISCONTINUED.

MY BACK! MY WOUND IS KILLING ME! PLEASE, PLEASE STOP THIS!

THE CIA REPRESENTED THAT ZUBAYDAH'S RECOVERY FROM HIS WOUND WOULD NOT BE IMPEDED BY THE USE OF EITS. BUT THEY LATER CONFIRMED THAT THE INTERROGATION PROCESS WOULD TAKE PRECEDENCE OVER PREVENTION OF HIS WOUND BEING FURTHER INFECTED.

OTHER DETAINEES WERE SUBJECTED TO EITS NOTWITHSTANDING CONCERNS THAT THEIR INJURIES COULD GET WORSE.

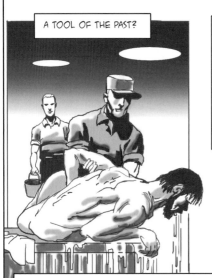

A TOOL OF THE PAST?

ON MAY 24, 2004, AFTER QUESTIONS AROSE ABOUT THE CONSTITUTIONAL LEGALITY OF EITS, CIA DIRECTOR GEORGE TENET SUSPENDED THEIR USE PENDING POLICY AND LEGAL REVIEW. AFTER FURTHER REVIEWS, ON JULY 22, 2004, ATTORNEY GENERAL JOHN ASHCROFT DECLARED NINE TECHNIQUES (THE WATERBOARD NOW AN EXCEPTION) DID NOT VIOLATE THE CONSTITUTION OR ANY STATUTE OR TREATY OBLIGATION AND COULD BE USED IN THE INTERROGATION OF JANAT GUL.

ON JULY 30, 2004, ANTICIPATING THE INTERROGATION OF GUL, THE CIA PROVIDED, FOR THE FIRST TIME, DESCRIPTIONS OF DIET MANIPULATION, NUDITY, WATER DOUSING, THE ABDOMINAL SLAP, STANDING SLEEP DEPRIVATION, AND THE USE OF DIAPERS. THE DESCRIPTIONS OF THE TECHNIQUES WERE INCONGRUENT WITH HOW THEY HAD BEEN APPLIED IN PRACTICE.

THE CIA DESCRIPTION OF A REDUCED CALORIE INTAKE WAS NEW AND HAD NOT EXISTED BEFORE. NUDE DETAINEES WERE NOT TO BE "WANTONLY EXPOSED TO OTHER DETAINEES," EVEN THOUGH THEY WERE "WALKED AROUND" BY GUARDS AS A FORM OF HUMILIATION. A TWO-HOUR LIMIT WAS SET FOR THE SHACKLING OF DETAINEES' HANDS ABOVE THEIR HEADS, WHILE THERE HAD BEEN NO LIMIT BEFORE. AND THE USE OF DIAPERS WAS "FOR SANITATION AND HYGIENE PURPOSES," WHEREAS CIA RECORDS INDICATE THAT, IN SOME CASES, THE CENTRAL "PURPOSE" OF DIAPERS WAS "TO CAUSE HUMILIATION" AND "INDUCE A SENSE OF HELPLESSNESS."

ON AUGUST 25, 2004, THE CIA'S ASSOCIATE GENERAL COUNSEL WROTE THE OLC, STATING THAT JANAT GUL HAD BEEN SUBJECTED TO THE ATTENTION GRAB, WALLING, FACIAL HOLD, FACIAL SLAP, WALL STANDING, STRESS POSITIONS, AND SLEEP DEPRIVATION, AND APPEARED "NOT TO BE COOPERATING, AND TO BE USING A SOPHISTICATED COUNTERINTERROGATION STRATEGY."

AND THAT USING THE SAME EITS WOULD BE "UNLIKELY TO MOVE GUL TO COOPERATE."

I SWEAR I KNOW NOTHING MORE.

SIGNIFICANT SWELLING OF HIS LEGS FROM STANDING SLEEP DEPRIVATION.

ONE DAY LATER, ACTING ASSISTANT ATTORNEY GENERAL DANIEL LEVIN INFORMED CIA ACTING GENERAL COUNSEL JOHN RIZZO THAT USE OF THE FOUR ADDITIONAL TECHNIQUES DID NOT VIOLATE ANY U.S. STATUTES. HIS ADVICE RELIED ON THE CIA'S REPRESENTATIONS ABOUT GUL'S HEALTH THAT "THERE ARE NO MEDICAL AND PSYCHOLOGICAL CONTRADICTIONS TO [THEIR] USE." HOWEVER, CIA RECORDS INDICATED THAT CIA INTERROGATORS BELIEVED THIS WOULD NOT PRODUCE ANY MORE INFORMATION NOR WAS GUL WITHHOLDING ANY.

IS THAT YOU, ALLAH? PLEASE TELL ME IT IS YOU!

IN NOVEMBER 2004, AFTER THE USE OF EITS ON GUL, THE CHIEF OF THE BASE WHERE HE HAD BEEN INTERROGATED WROTE, "DESCRIBING GUL AS 'HIGHEST RANKING' GIVES HIM A STATURE THAT IS UNDESERVED, OVERBLOWN, AND MISLEADING."

AND I THOUGHT WE HAD A HOME RUN WITH HIM!

IN DECEMBER 2004, CIA OFFICERS CONCLUDED THAT GUL WAS "NOT THE LINK TO SENIOR AQ LEADERS THAT [CIA HEADQUARTERS] SAID HE WAS."

AND IN APRIL 2005, CIA OFFICERS WROTE, "THERE SIMPLY IS NO 'SMOKING GUN' THAT WE CAN REFER TO THAT WOULD JUSTIFY OUR CONTINUED HOLDING OF" GUL.

YET, IN A MAY 30, 2005, MEMO, THE OLC CALLED JANAT GUL "REPRESENTATIVE OF THE HIGH-VALUE DETAINEES ON WHOM ENHANCED TECHNIQUES HAVE BEEN, OR MIGHT BE USED" AND THAT "THE CIA BELIEVED [THAT GUL] HAD ACTIONABLE INTELLIGENCE CONCERNING THE PRE-ELECTION THREAT TO THE UNITED STATES." THE MEMO ALSO STATED...

GUL HAS PRODUCED INFORMATION THAT HAS HELPED THE CIA WITH VALIDATING ONE OF ITS KEY ASSETS REPORTING ON THE PRE-ELECTION THREAT . . .

THERE ARE NO INDICATIONS IN THE MEMO THAT THE CIA INFORMED THE OLC THAT IT HAD CONCLUDED THAT GUL HAD NO INFORMATION ABOUT THE PRE-ELECTION THREAT, WHICH WAS THE BASIS FOR THE USE OF EITS.

I COULD NOT MARRY YOU, MARIA, MY FATHER WOULD HAVE DISOWNED ME. BUT I STILL LOVE YOU . . .

IN SEPTEMBER 2004, THE OLC ALLOWED THE CIA TO USE EITS AGAINST AHMED KHALFAN GHAILANI AND SHARIF AL-MASRI, BASED ON REPRESENTATIONS THEY WERE AL-QA'IDA OPERATIVES INVOLVED IN THE PRE-ELECTION PLOT AGAINST THE UNITED STATES. BOTH WERE SUBJECTED TO EXTENDED SLEEP DEPRIVATION AND EXPERIENCED HALLUCINATIONS.

THIS DECISION WAS BASED ON THE SAME FABRICATIONS FROM THE SAME CIA SOURCE THAT CITED GUL.

ON MAY 4, 2005, ASSISTANT ATTORNEY GENERAL STEVEN BRADBURY QUESTIONED THE CIA ABOUT ITS EITS. THEY RESPONDED THAT ANY LOWERING OF THE THRESHOLD OF PAIN WAS "NOT GERMANE" TO THE PROGRAM AS STUDIES HAD ONLY IDENTIFIED DIFFERENCES IN SENSITIVITY TO HEAT, COLD, PRESSURE, ANY SHARP OBJECTS, OR ANY OBJECTS AT ALL. AS TO THE EFFECT OF SLEEP DEPRIVATION IN THE USE OF WATER DOUSINGS, THE RESPONSE STATED, "AT THE TEMPERATURES OF WATER WE HAVE RECOMMENDED FOR THE PROGRAM THE LIKELIHOOD OF . . . PAIN BY WATER DOUSING IS VERY LOW UNDER ANY CIRCUMSTANCES."

THEY ALSO DID NOT BELIEVE THAT SIGNIFICANT SWELLING OF THE LOWER EXTREMITIES (EDEMA) OR SHACKLING WOULD BE MORE PAINFUL PROVIDED THE SHACKLES WERE MAINTAINED WITH "APPROPRIATE SLACK." AND THAT "DETAINEES HAVE NOT COMPLAINED ABOUT PAIN FROM EDEMA." MUCH OF THIS INFORMATION IS INACCURATE.

I'M DYING! I'M DYING! PLEASE STOP!

THINK HE'S GOT TOO MUCH PAIN?

LET'S GIVE IT ANOTHER 15 MINUTES!

ASSISTANT ATTORNEY GENERAL STEVEN BRADBURY ASKED WHETHER IT WAS "POSSIBLE TO TELL RELIABLY (E.G., FROM OUTWARD PHYSICAL SIGNS LIKE GRIMACES) WHETHER A DETAINEE IS EXPERIENCING SEVERE PAIN." THE CIA RESPONDED THAT "ALL PAIN IS SUBJECTIVE, NOT OBJECTIVE, . . . [AND] MEDICAL OFFICERS CAN MONITOR FOR EVIDENCE OF CONDITION OR INJURY."

MULTIPLE CIA DETAINEES WERE SUBJECTED TO EITS DESPITE THEIR MEDICAL CONDITION.

BRADBURY THEN ASKED WHETHER MONITORING AND SAFEGUARDS "WILL EFFECTIVELY AVOID SEVERE PHYSICAL PAIN OR SUFFERING FOR DETAINEES." THE CIA RESPONDED . . .

APPLICATION OF THE THIRTEEN TECHNIQUES HAS NOT TO DATE RESULTED IN ANY SEVERE OR PERMANENT PHYSICAL INJURY, OTHER THAN TRANSIENT BRUISING . . . AND WE DO NOT EXPECT THIS TO CHANGE.

BRADBURY THEN SIGNED THREE MEMORANDA THAT RELIED ON INFORMATION PROVIDED BY THE CIA--THAT WAS INCONSISTENT WITH CIA RECORDS-- AND APPROVED THE USE OF ALL THIRTEEN EITS.

GOOD TO BE BACK IN ACTION AGAIN!

HE WAS TOLD THESE TECHNIQUES WOULD BE USED ONLY WHEN THE INTERROGATION TEAM "CONSIDERS THEM NECESSARY BECAUSE A DETAINEE IS WITHHOLDING . . . INTELLIGENCE"; IT WILL BE "DISCONTINUED IF THE DETAINEE IS JUDGED TO BE . . . PROVIDING ACCURATE INTELLIGENCE OR . . . IS NO LONGER BELIEVED TO HAVE ACTIONABLE INTELLIGENCE."

IT ENDS "WHEN THE DETAINEE BEGINS PARTICIPATING"; "WOULD NOT BE USED ON A DETAINEE NOT REASONABLY THOUGHT TO POSSESS IMPORTANT ACTIONABLE INTELLIGENCE"; AND THE PROCESS BEGINS WITH "AN OPEN, NON-THREATENING APPROACH."

THIS IS THE C-C-COLDEST 75 DEGREES I'VE EVER F-F-FELT!

THE OLC MEMORANDA RELIED ON CIA REPRESENTATIONS REGARDING SPECIFIC TECHNIQUES THAT WERE INCONGRUENT WITH THE OPERATIONAL HISTORY OF THE PROGRAM. FOR EXAMPLE, THEY CLAIMED IT KEPT A 75-DEGREE ROOM TEMPERATURE FOR NUDE DETAINEES AS A "MATTER OF POLICY."

THIS INFORMATION WAS INCONSISTENT WITH CIA PRACTICE BOTH BEFORE AND AFTER THE CIA CLAIM TO THE OLC.

ALLAH HELP ME . . .

DON'T LOOK! AN AGENT ON THE OUTSIDE IS LOOKING.

THE CIA REPRESENTED THAT STANDING SLEEP DEPRIVATION WOULD BE DISCONTINUED IF THE DETAINEE HAD EDEMA.

IN PRACTICE, THE TECHNIQUE WAS REPEATEDLY NOT STOPPED WHEN EDEMA OCCURRED.

THE PAIN DOES NOT STOP!

THE OLC REPEATED CIA REPRESENTATIONS THAT CONSTANT LIGHT WAS NECESSARY FOR SECURITY, ALTHOUGH THE CIA HAD SUBJECTED DETAINEES TO CONSTANT DARKNESS. ADDITIONAL REPRESENTATIONS WERE THAT THEY EXPOSED NUDE DETAINEES TO STAFF AND OTHER DETAINEES, THEY USED SHACKLES DURING STANDING SLEEP DEPRIVATION, AND MEDICAL STAFF DID NOT INTERVENE WHEN HALLUCINATIONS OCCURRED.

THE OLC ACCEPTED THE CIA'S WORD THAT PHYSICAL SENSATIONS ASSOCIATED WITH WATERBOARDING SUCH AS CHOKING "END WHEN THE APPLICATION ENDS." THIS IS INCONGRUENT WITH CIA RECORDS. ACCORDING TO THOSE RECORDS, ABU ZUBAYDAH'S SESSION "RESULTED IN IMMEDIATE FLUID INTAKE AND INVOLUNTARY LEG, CHEST, AND ARM SPASMS" AND "HYSTERICAL PLEAS."

A MEDICAL OFFICER WHO OVERSAW THE INTERROGATION OF KSM STATED THAT THE TECHNIQUE EVOLVED BEYOND THE "SENSATION OF DROWNING" TO "A SERIES OF NEAR DROWNINGS." DURING ONE SESSION, ZUBAYDAH "BECAME COMPLETELY UNRESPONSIVE, WITH BUBBLES RISING THROUGH HIS OPEN, FULL MOUTH."

NOW AS FAR AS THAT TOR-- UH, ENHANCED TECHNIQUE CALLED STANDING SLEET DEPRI--

STANDING *SLEEP* DEPRIVATION.

WHICH OF THE TECHNIQUES DO YOU THINK IS THE SAFEST AND MOST PROFESSIONAL?

I GUESS HE'S AN AL-QA'IDA MEMBER.

WELL, THE AGENT IN CHARGE SAID HE MUMBLED THAT HE WAS A MEMBER OF THE ODD FELLOWS, PROBABLY THE TRANSLATION OF AL-QA'IDA.

A MAY 10, 2005, OLC MEMO ANALYZING THE INDIVIDUAL USE OF THE CIA'S EITS ACCEPTED THE CIA CLAIM THAT INTERROGATORS ARE TRAINED FOR "APPROXIMATELY FOUR WEEKS" AND "ALL PERSONNEL DIRECTLY ENGAGED . . . HAVE BEEN APPROPRIATELY SCREENED (FROM MEDICAL, PSYCHOLOGICAL AND SECURITY STANDPOINTS)."

BUT THE CIA REPRESENTATIONS WERE INCONGRUENT WITH THE OPERATION AND HISTORY OF THE PROGRAM. THE CIA OFFICERS AND CONTRACTORS WHO CONDUCTED INTERROGATION IN 2002 DID *NOT* UNDERGO ANY INTERROGATION TRAINING.

ON MARCH 2, 2005, THE CIA ISSUED THE SO-CALLED EFFECTIVENESS MEMO, ADVISING THAT THE CIA'S ENHANCED INTERROGATION "WORKS AND THE TECHNIQUES ARE EFFECTIVE IN PRODUCING FOREIGN INTELLIGENCE." IT CLAIMS "WE WOULD NOT HAVE SUCCEEDED IN OVERCOMING THE RESISTANCE OF KSM, ABU ZUBAYDAH, AND OTHER EQUALLY RESISTANT HIGH-VALUE TERRORIST DETAINEES WITHOUT APPLYING, IN A CAREFUL, PROFESSIONAL, AND SAFE MANNER, THE FULL RANGE OF INTERROGATION TECHNIQUES."

HOWEVER, THE KEY INFORMATION PROVIDED BY ZUBAYDAH WAS PROVIDED PRIOR TO THE USE OF EITS. AND KSM WAS SUBJECTED TO EITS WITHIN MINUTES OF HIS QUESTIONING AND HAD NO CHANCE TO DIVULGE INFORMATION PRIOR TO THEIR USE.

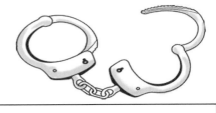

THE OLC ACCEPTED THE CIA REPRESENTATION THAT EITS WERE LIMITED TO "SENIOR MEMBERS" OF AL-QA'IDA OR AN ASSOCIATED TERRORIST GROUP, WHO HAVE "KNOWLEDGE OF IMMINENT TERRORIST THREATS" OR "DIRECT INVOLVEMENT IN PLANNING AND PREPARING TERRORIST ACTIONS."

HOWEVER, AT THAT TIME, THE CIA HAD USED THESE TECHNIQUES ON DETAINEES WHO WERE FOUND NEITHER TO HAVE KNOWLEDGE OF IMMINENT THREATS NOR TO BE INVOLVED IN PLANNING OR PREPARING TERRORIST ACTIONS. SOME WERE NOT SENIOR AL-QA'IDA MEMBERS OR MEMBERS AT ALL.

REVIEW OF CIA REPRESENTATIONS TO CONGRESS

UNDER A SECTION ENTITLED "RESULTS," THE EFFECTIVENESS MEMO STATED THAT THE "CIA'S USE OF DOJ-APPROVED ENHANCED INTERROGATION TECHNIQUES . . . HAS ENABLED THE CIA TO DISRUPT TERRORIST PLOTS, CAPTURE ADDITIONAL TERRORISTS, AND COLLECT A HIGH VOLUME OF CRITICAL INTELLIGENCE ON AL-QA'IDA."

THEY THEN LISTED 11 EXAMPLES OF "CRITICAL INTELLIGENCE" IT ACQUIRED. THESE REPRESENTATIONS WERE ALMOST ENTIRELY INACCURATE AND MIRRORED OTHER INACCURATE INFORMATION PROVIDED TO THE WHITE HOUSE, CONGRESS, AND THE CIA INSPECTOR GENERAL.

THE OLC'S MAY 30, 2005, MEMO RELIED ON THE CIA'S INACCURATE REPRESENTATIONS IN THE EFFECTIVENESS MEMO AND THE "BRIEFING NOTES" IN DETERMINING THAT EITS DID NOT VIOLATE THE FIFTH AMENDMENT'S PROHIBITION OF EXECUTIVE CONDUCT THAT "SHOCKS THE CONSCIENCE," INDICATING THAT THIS ANALYSIS WAS A "HIGHLY CONTEXT-SPECIFIC AND FACT-DEPENDENT QUESTION."

THE MEMO REPEATED SPECIFIC INACCURATE CIA REPRESENTATIONS, INCLUDING THAT THE WATERBOARD WAS USED AGAINST ZUBAYDAH AND KSM "ONLY AFTER IT BECAME CLEAR THAT STANDARD INTERROGATION TECHNIQUES WERE NOT WORKING," THAT JANAT GUL WAS A "HIGH-VALUE DETAINEE," AND THAT INFORMATION PROVIDED BY HASSAN GHUL REGARDING THE AL-QA'IDA PRESENCE IN SHKAI, PAKISTAN, WAS ATTRIBUTABLE TO THE USE OF EITS.

THE OLC REPEATED ADDITIONAL INACCURATE INFORMATION FROM THE CIA RELATED TO KSM'S REPORTING ABOUT THE SECOND WAVE PLOT, THE HEATHROW AIRPORT PLOT, AND THE CAPTURES OF HAMBALI, IYMAN FARIS, AND SAJID BADAT.

AND THAT USING EITS ON ABD AL-RAHIM AL-NASHIRI PRODUCED "NOTABLE RESULTS," DESPITE HIS PROVIDING THE SAME INFORMATION PRIOR TO BEING IN CIA CUSTODY.

EVEN AS THE OLC WITHDREW A DRAFT OPINION ON THE CIA'S EITS, THEY CONTINUED TO ANALYZE WHETHER THEIR CONDITIONS OF CONFINEMENT VIOLATED THE DETAINEE TREATMENT ACT. IN ITS DEFENSE, THE CIA ASSERTED THAT LOUD MUSIC AND WHITE NOISE, CONSTANT LIGHT, AND 24-HOUR SHACKLING WERE ALL FOR SECURITY PURPOSES; SHAVING WAS FOR SECURITY AND HYGIENE PURPOSES; AND THAT DETAINEES HAD ACCESS TO A WIDE ARRAY OF AMENITIES.

ALL THIS IS INCONGRUENT WITH CIA RECORDS.

DETAINEES WERE ROUTINELY SHAVED, SOMETIMES AS AN AID TO INTERROGATION.

DETAINEES WHO WERE "PARTICIPATING AT AN ACCEPTABLE LEVEL" WERE PERMITTED TO GROW THEIR HAIR AND BEARDS.

THE CIA USED MUSIC AT DECIBELS EXCEEDING THE REPRESENTATIONS TO THE OLC, AND NUMEROUS DETAINEES WERE SUBJECTED TO THE CONTINUED USE OF WHITE NOISE.

ON AUGUST 31, 2006, THE OLC WROTE THAT "UNDERLYING OUR ANALYSIS OF ALL THESE [CONDITIONS OF CONFINEMENT] IS OUR UNDERSTANDING THAT THE CIA PROVIDES REGULAR AND THOROUGH MEDICAL AND PSYCHOLOGICAL CARE TO THE DETAINEES."

AS MENTIONED BEFORE, THE LACK OF EMERGENCY MEDICAL CARE FOR CIA DETAINEES WAS A SIGNIFICANT CHALLENGE TO THE CIA.

THE AUGUST 31, 2006, MEMO CITED THAT THE CIA HAD DETAINED "A TOTAL OF 96 INDIVIDUALS," WHEN, AT THE TIME, THE CIA HAD ACTUALLY DETAINED AT LEAST 118. THE MEMO ALSO STATES THAT WHEN "A DETAINEE NO LONGER POSSESSES SIGNIFICANT INTELLIGENCE VALUE . . . THE DETAINEE [IS MOVED] INTO ALTERNATIVE DETENTION ARRANGEMENTS."

CIA RECORDS INDICATE THAT DETAINEES REMAINED IN CUSTODY LONG AFTER THE CIA DETERMINED THEY POSSESSED NO SIGNIFICANT INFORMATION.

ON JULY 20, 2007, THE OLC DETERMINED THAT SIX INTERROGATION TECHNIQUES WERE LEGAL. THESE WERE DIETARY MANIPULATION, EXTENDED SLEEP DEPRIVATION, THE FACIAL HOLD, THE ATTENTION GRASP, THE ABDOMINAL SLAP, AND THE FACIAL SLAP. THEY ALSO ACCEPTED THE CIA'S CLAIM THAT THEY HAD DETAINED 98 INDIVIDUALS, OF WHICH 30 HAD BEEN SUBJECTED TO EITS.

THE CIA HAD ACTUALLY DETAINED AT LEAST 119 INDIVIDUALS, OF WHICH AT LEAST 38 HAD BEEN SUBJECTED TO EITS. THE INACCURATE STATISTICS WERE USED TO SUPPORT THE OLC'S CONCLUSION THAT THE PROGRAM WAS "PROPORTIONATE TO THE GOVERNMENT INTEREST INVOLVED" AS REQUIRED BY THE "SHOCKS THE CONSCIENCE" TEST.

YES, I THINK HE IS A MEMBER OF AL-QA'IDA.

THINK?

THE OLC ALSO NOTED "CAREFUL SCREENING PROCEDURES ARE IN PLACE TO ENSURE THAT ENHANCED TECHNIQUES WILL BE USED ONLY IN THE INTERROGATIONS OF AGENTS OR MEMBERS OF AL-QA'IDA OR ITS AFFILIATES WHO ARE REASONABLY BELIEVED TO POSSESS CRITICAL INTELLIGENCE THAT CAN BE USED TO PREVENT FUTURE TERRORIST ATTACKS AGAINST THE UNITED STATES AND ITS INTERESTS."

IN PRACTICE, NUMEROUS INDIVIDUALS WERE DETAINED BY THE CIA AND SUBJECTED TO EITS DESPITE DOUBTS AND QUESTIONS ABOUT THEIR KNOWLEDGE OF ATTACKS OR TIES TO AL-QA'IDA, SUCH AS ASADULLAH, ARSALA KHAN, JANAT GUL, AND SAYYID IBRAHIM.

ALRIGHT! I'LL TELL YOU EVERYTHING!

HRRRGHH!

STOP THE WATERBOARDING IMMEDIATELY.

THE OLC ACCEPTED THE CIA'S REPRESENTATION THAT "THE CIA GENERALLY DOES NOT ASK QUESTIONS DURING THE ADMINISTRATION OF THE TECHNIQUES TO WHICH THE CIA DOES NOT ALREADY KNOW THE ANSWERS." AND WHEN THEY BELIEVE A DETAINEE WILL COOPERATE, THEY WILL STOP THE USE OF THE TECHNIQUE AND DEBRIEF THE DETAINEE.

THIS DESCRIPTION OF THE PROGRAM IS INACCURATE. CIA INTERROGATORS ALWAYS QUESTIONED DETAINEES DURING THE APPLICATION OF A TECHNIQUE.

STOP! I WILL TELL YOU WHAT YOU WANT! AND WITH A CLEAR CONSCIENCE!

THE JULY 20, 2007, OLC MEMO REPEATED CIA REPRESENTATIONS THAT "MANY, IF NOT ALL, OF THOSE 30 DETAINEES" SUBJECTED TO THE CIA'S EITS RECEIVED COUNTERINTERROGATION TRAINING AND THAT "AL-QA'IDA OPERATIVES BELIEVE THAT THEY ARE MORALLY PERMITTED TO REVEAL INFORMATION ONCE THEY HAVE REACHED A CERTAIN LEVEL OF DISCOMFORT."

NONE OF THIS IS SUPPORTED BY CIA RECORDS.

THE PSYCHIATRIST WHO TAUGHT ME SAID THAT WHEN THIS HAPPENS, DON'T INTERFERE.

GOOD MORNING, *BABY!*

THE BELIEF THAT THE CIA REPRESENTATIONS WERE ACCURATE IN CLAIMING THAT THE INTERROGATORS WERE HIGHLY TRAINED IN THE TECHNIQUES AND PSYCHOLOGICALLY SCREENED TO NOT MISUSE THEM WERE CENTRAL TO THE OLC'S TRUST IN THE PROGRAM. HOWEVER, THE CIA REPRESENTATIONS WERE INCONGRUENT WITH THEIR RECORDS.

IN REVIEWING WHETHER STANDING SLEEP DEPRIVATION WAS CONSISTENT WITH THE WAR CRIMES ACT, THE OLC NOTED THAT THE CIA SAID THE TECHNIQUES WOULD BE DISCONTINUED "SHOULD ANY HALLUCINATIONS OR SIGNIFICANT DECLINES IN COGNITIVE FUNCTIONING BE OBSERVED." THE MEMO ALSO MENTIONED THAT DIAPERS USED DURING STANDING SLEEP DEPRIVATION "ARE USED SOLELY FOR SANITARY AND HEALTH REASONS AND NOT TO HUMILIATE." THIS WAS NOT CONSISTENT WITH THE OPERATIONAL HISTORY OF THE CIA PROGRAM.

THESE TECHNIQUES ARE TORTURE!

FINALLY, THAT OLC MEMO ASSERTED THAT MEMBERS OF CONGRESS, INCLUDING THE HOUSE AND SEN-ATE INTELLIGENCE COMMITTEES, SUPPORTED THE CIA INTERROGATION PROGRAM. NOT SO! SENATOR JOHN MCCAIN INFORMED THE CIA HE BELIEVED THE TECHNIQUES WERE "TORTURE."

SENATOR DIANNE FEINSTEIN WROTE CIA DIRECTOR MICHAEL HAYDEN THAT SHE WAS "UNABLE TO UNDERSTAND WHY THE CIA NEEDS TO MAINTAIN THIS PROGRAM."

SENATOR RUSS FEINGOLD WROTE, "I CANNOT SUPPORT THIS PROGRAM ON MORAL, LEGAL, OR NATIONAL SECURITY GROUNDS." SENATORS CHUCK HAGEL AND RON WYDEN ECHOED THE SAME.

SENATOR DIANNE FEINSTEIN

THEIR NEW AUTHORITIES ARE *TERRIFYING!*

DEPUTY DIRECTOR OF OPERATION JAMES PAVITT

FOLLOWING THE 9/11 ATTACKS IN 2001 AND THE SIGNING ON SEPTEMBER 17, 2001, OF THE MEMORANDUM OF NOTIFICATION (MON), THE SSCI HELD A SERIES OF HEARINGS AND BRIEFINGS ON CIA COVERT ACTIONS, INCLUDING THE NEW AUTHORITY TO DETAIN TERRORISTS. AT A NOVEMBER 13, 2001, BRIEFING, THE COMMITTEE STAFF DESCRIBED THE NEW DETENTION AUTHORITIES AS "TERRIFYING" AND EXPRESSED THE CIA'S INTENT TO "FIND A CADRE OF PEOPLE WHO KNOW HOW TO RUN PRISONS, BECAUSE WE DON'T."

HE'S AGAINST TORTURE, BUT IN FAVOR OF THOSE TECHNIQUES?

DEPUTY DIRECTOR OF OPERATION JAMES PAVITT ASSURED THE COMMITTEE IT WOULD BE INFORMED OF EACH INDIVIDUAL WHO ENTERED CIA CUSTODY. HE DISAVOWED THE USE OF TORTURE AGAINST DETAINEES WHILE STATING THAT THE BOUNDARIES ON THE USE OF INTERROGATION TECHNIQUES WERE UNCERTAIN—SPECIFICALLY IN THE CASE OF IDENTIFYING THE LOCATION OF A HIDDEN NUCLEAR WEAPON.

AND THE CIA HAS NO PLANS TO DEVELOP A DETENTION FACILITY.

ON APRIL 18, 2002, THE CIA INFORMED THE COMMITTEE THAT IT "HAS NO CURRENT PLANS TO DEVELOP A DETENTION FACILITY." AT THAT TIME, THE CIA HAD ALREADY CREATED A CIA DETENTION SITE IN AN UNNAMED COUNTRY AND DETAINED ABU ZUBAYDAH THERE. ON APRIL 24, 2002, THE CIA NOTIFIED THE COMMITTEE ABOUT HIS CAPTURE WITH THE UNDERSTANDING THAT THE LOCATION OF HIS DETENTION WOULD NOT BE DIVULGED TO THEM. THE NOTIFICATION AND SUBSEQUENT INFORMATION GIVEN INCLUDED REPRESENTATIONS THAT ZUBAYDAH WAS A "MEMBER OF BIN LADEN'S INNER CIRCLE" AND A "KEY AL-QA'IDA LIEUTENANT."

THESE REPRESENTATIONS WERE INACCURATE.

BRIEFINGS TO THE COMMITTEE IN SPRING OF 2002 EMPHASIZED THE EXPERTISE OF FBI AND CIA INTERROGATORS ENGAGED IN THE ABU ZUBAYDAH INTERROGATIONS AND PROVIDED NO INDICATION THAT COERCIVE TECHNIQUES WERE BEING USED OR CONSIDERED OR THAT THERE WAS SIGNIFICANT DISAGREEMENT BETWEEN THE TWO ORGANIZATIONS ON PROPOSED INTERROGATION APPROACHES.

IN EARLY AUGUST 2002, AFTER THE DEPARTMENT OF JUSTICE DETERMINED THE USE OF THE CIA'S EITS WAS LEGAL, THE CIA CONSIDERED BRIEFING THE COMMITTEE ON THE TECHNIQUES, BUT DID NOT.

THE FIRST BRIEFING OF THE SSCI CHAIRMAN BOB GRAHAM AND VICE CHAIRMAN RICHARD SHELBY AND THEIR STAFF OCCURRED ON SEPTEMBER 27, 2002, NEARLY TWO MONTHS AFTER THE CIA BEGAN SUBJECTING ZUBAYDAH TO EITS. THE ONLY RECORD OF THE BRIEFING IS A ONE-PARAGRAPH CIA MEMO STATING IT HAD OCCURRED.

SHORTLY THEREAFTER, IN LATE 2002, CHAIRMAN GRAHAM SOUGHT TO EXPAND COMMITTEE OVERSIGHT OF THE DETENTION AND INTERROGATION PROGRAM BY HAVING STAFF VISIT CIA INTERROGATION SITES AND INTERVIEW INTERROGATORS.

THE CIA REJECTED THE PROPOSAL.

AN INTERNAL CIA E-MAIL AT THE TIME INDICATED THAT THE FULL COMMITTEE WOULD NOT BE TOLD ABOUT "THE NATURE AND SCOPE OF THE INTERROGATION PROCESS." EVEN THE CHAIRMAN AND VICE CHAIRMAN WOULD NOT BE TOLD IN WHICH COUNTRY OR REGION THE CIA HAD ESTABLISHED ITS DETENTION FACILITIES.

SEVERAL E-MAILS DESCRIBE EFFORTS BY THE CIA TO FORMULATE A "STRATEGY" FOR LIMITING CIA RESPONSES TO GRAHAM'S REQUEST FOR MORE INFORMATION ON THE DETENTION AND INTERROGATION PROGRAM. THE CIA FINALLY CHOSE TO DELAY ITS NEXT UPDATE UNTIL GRAHAM HAD LEFT THE COMMITTEE.

THROUGHOUT 2003, THE CIA REFUSED TO ANSWER QUESTIONS FROM COMMITTEE MEMBERS ABOUT THEIR INTERROGATION OF KSM AND OTHER DETAINEES. THEY CONTINUED TO WITHHOLD INFORMATION FROM EVEN THE COMMITTEE LEADERSHIP ON THE LOCATION OF ITS DETENTION FACILITIES AND THE LEGALITY OF ITS INTERROGATION PROGRAM.

ON MAY 12, 2004, THE COMMITTEE REQUESTED TO VIEW A DEPARTMENT OF JUSTICE MEMO ADDRESSING THE LEGALITY OF ITS INTERROGATION PROCESS. NOT UNTIL JUNE 2008 WAS IT SHOWN TO THEM, AT WHICH TIME THE CIA WAS NO LONGER DETAINING INDIVIDUALS.

CIA DESTRUCTION OF INTERROGATION VIDEOS

AND IF THIS DOESN'T SHUT HIM UP . . .

ON MARCH 3, 2005, A CIA OFFICIAL WROTE THAT VICE CHAIRMAN JOHN D. ROCKEFELLER WAS "CONVINCED THAT WE'RE HIDING STUFF FROM HIM" AND THAT THE CIA PLANNED A DETAILED BRIEFING TO "SHUT ROCKEFELLER UP."

SHORTLY AFTER THIS BRIEFING, ROCKEFELLER REITERATED HIS CALL FOR A BROAD COMMITTEE INVESTIGATION OF THE CIA'S INTERROGATION PROGRAM, WHICH HE AND RANKING MEMBER OF THE HOUSE PERMANENT SELECT COMMITTEE ON INTELLIGENCE (HPSCI) JANE HARMAN DESCRIBED IN A LETTER TO VICE PRESIDENT DICK CHENEY, WHICH WAS NEVER ANSWERED.

THERE'S TALK ABOUT DESTROYING THEM!

IN 2005, SENATOR CARL LEVIN'S PROPOSAL TO CREATE AN INDEPENDENT COMMISSION TO INVESTIGATE U.S. DETENTION POLICIES AND ALLEGATIONS OF DETAINEE ABUSE RESULTED IN CONCERN AT THE CIA ABOUT THEIR VIDEOTAPES OF INTERROGATIONS. THIS PROMPTED RENEWED CIA INTEREST IN DESTROYING THE TAPES.

SENATOR LEVIN'S AMENDMENT, HOWEVER, FAILED TO PASS ON NOVEMBER 8, 2005.

THE CIA DESTROYED THE TAPES THE FOLLOWING DAY.

IN MARCH 2006, THREE MONTHS AFTER PASSAGE OF THE DETAINEE TREATMENT ACT, THE CIA BRIEFED COMMITTEE STAFFERS, INCLUDING LIMITED INFORMATION ON THE INTERROGATION PROCESS AS WELL AS ITS EFFECTIVENESS. CIA DIRECTOR PORTER GOSS DECLARED . . .

THIS PROGRAM HAS BROUGHT US INCREDIBLE INFORMATION . . . [AND] COULD CONTINUE TO BRING US INCREDIBLE INFORMATION . . . YOU WOULD BE PROUD THAT IT'S DONE RIGHT AND WELL, WITH PROPER SAFEGUARDS.

HE THEN REPRESENTED THAT THE DETAINMENT AND INTERROGATION PROGRAM IS "NOT A BRUTALITY. IT'S MORE OF AN ART OR A SCIENCE THAT IS REFINED."

EXAMPLES OF INACCURATE TESTIMONY TO THE SSCI PART I

IN MAY 2006, THE SSCI APPROVED LEGISLATION REQUIRING THE CIA TO PROVIDE REPORTS ON ITS DETENTION FACILITIES (INCLUDING THEIR LOCATIONS), THE CIA INTERROGATION TECHNIQUES, THE IMPACT OF THE DETAINEE TREATMENT ACT ON THE CIA PROGRAM, AND CIA RENDITIONS AND PLANS FOR THE DISPOSITION OF ITS DETAINEES. IT ALSO CALLED FOR FULL COMMITTEE ACCESS TO THE CIA AS WELL AS EXPANDED COMMITTEE STAFF ACCESS TO THE DETENTION AND INTERROGATION PROGRAM.

NOW TO SEE HOW FAR IT GOES.

TO WIN THE WAR ON TERROR, WE MUST BE ABLE TO DETAIN, QUESTION, AND, WHEN APPROPRIATE, PROSECUTE TERRORISTS . . .

ON SEPTEMBER 6, 2006, PRESIDENT BUSH PUBLICLY ACKNOWLEDGED THE CIA PROGRAM AND THE TRANSFER OF 14 CIA DETAINEES TO U.S. MILITARY CUSTODY AT GUANTANAMO BAY, CUBA. HOURS PRIOR TO THE ANNOUNCEMENT, CIA DIRECTOR MICHAEL HAYDEN PROVIDED THE FIRST BRIEFING ON THE CIA'S ENHANCED INTERROGATION PROGRAM FOR ALL MEMBERS OF THE COMMITTEE––ALTHOUGH THE CIA LIMITED STAFF ATTENDANCE TO THE COMMITTEE'S TWO STAFF DIRECTORS.

THE CIA'S EITS WERE LISTED BUT NOT DESCRIBED. DIRECTOR HAYDEN STATED THEY WERE DEVELOPED AT THE SERE SCHOOL AND "USED AGAINST AMERICAN SERVICE PERSONNEL DURING THEIR TRAINING." HE TESTIFIED THAT "ONCE (A DETAINEE) GETS INTO THE SITUATION OF SUSTAINED COOPERATION," DEBRIEFINGS ARE "NOT SIGNIFICANTLY DIFFERENT THAN WHAT YOU AND I ARE DOING RIGHT NOW." HE HAD BEEN INFORMED INFORMALLY THAT SEVEN INTERROGATION TECHNIQUES "ARE VIEWED BY THE DEPARTMENT OF JUSTICE TO BE CONSISTENT WITH REQUIREMENTS OF THE DETAINEE TREATMENT ACT."

OK, STOP THIS DAMN THING! OR YOU'LL HAVE A DEAD GI TO DEAL WITH!

I CANNOT SUPPORT THIS PROGRAM AND BELIEVE THAT SLEEP DEPRIVATION AS WELL AS WATERBOARDING IS TORTURE!

JOHN MCCAIN

THE DEPARTMENT OF JUSTICE LATER CONCLUDED THAT THE CIA'S EITS WERE CONSISTENT WITH THE MILITARY COMMISSIONS ACT IN PART BECAUSE, ACCORDING TO THE CIA, "NONE OF THE MEMBERS EXPRESSED THE VIEW THAT THE CIA INTERROGATION PROGRAM SHOULD BE STOPPED, . . . OR THE TECHNIQUES INAPPROPRIATE." PRIOR TO THE VOTE, HOWEVER, SENATOR JOHN MCCAIN AND SENATOR DIANNE FEINSTEIN STRONGLY OBJECTED.

WE ARE LEFT WITH VERY LITTLE OFFENSE AND ARE RELEGATED TO RELY PRIMARILY ON DEFENSE.

CIA DIRECTOR MICHAEL HAYDEN'S STATEMENT ON APRIL 12, 2007, INCLUDED EXTENSIVE INACCURACIES WITH REGARD TO ABU ZUBAYDAH, CIA INTERROGATIONS, ABUSES IDENTIFIED BY THE ICRC, AND THE EFFECTIVENESS OF EITS. IN HIS STATEMENT REGARDING SUBSTITUTING THE ARMY FIELD MANUAL FOR EITS, HE SAID, "WITHOUT THE APPROVAL OF EITS . . . WE HAVE SEVERELY RESTRICTED OUR ATTEMPTS TO OBTAIN TIMELY INFORMATION . . . THAT WILL HELP US SAVE LIVES AND DISRUPT OPERATIONS."

IT WAS ABU ZUBAYDAH, EARLY IN HIS DETENTION, WHO IDENTIFIED KSM AS THE MASTERMIND OF 9/11. UNTIL THAT TIME, KSM DID NOT EVEN APPEAR IN OUR CHART OF KEY AL-QA'IDA MEMBERS.

ZUBAYDAH DID IDENTIFY HIM, BUT BEFORE EITS WERE USED ON HIM.

ON APRIL 12, 2007, IN A MEETING BETWEEN THE CIA AND THE SSCI, CIA DIRECTOR HAYDEN PROVIDED EXTENSIVE INACCURACIES REGARDING MANY TOPICS IN HIS ATTEMPT TO DEFEND HIS POSITION ON EITS.

OTHER INACCURACIES APPEARED IN DISCUSSIONS OF COUNTERINTERROGATION TRAINING, BACKGROUND OF CIA INTERROGATORS, NUMBER OF CIA DETAINEES, AND SO MUCH MORE.

MUHAMMAD RAHIM, CAPTURED IN AUGUST 2007, WAS ALLEGEDLY ONE OF BIN LADEN'S MOST TRUSTED FACILITATORS.

IN MAY 2007, THE COMMITTEE VOTED TO APPROVE THE FISCAL YEAR 2008 INTELLIGENCE AUTHORIZATION BILL, REQUIRING REPORTING ON CIA COMPLIANCE WITH THE DETAINEE TREATMENT ACT AND MILITARY COMMISSIONS ACT.

AND IN AUGUST, THE COMMITTEE ADDRESSED THE INTER-ROGATION OF RAHIM, THE CIA'S LAST DETAINEE, AS WELL AS THE PRESIDENT'S EXECUTIVE ORDER ALLOWING THE CIA TO USE THE ADVANCED TECHNIQUES ON RAHIM.

THE PRESIDENT'S EXPLANATIONS ECHOED THE CIA DECLARATIONS.

ON MARCH 8, 2008, PRESIDENT BUSH VETOED THE 2008 INTELLIGENCE AUTHORIZATION BILL THAT WOULD HAVE LIMITED CIA INTERROGATIONS TO TECHNIQUES AUTHORIZED BY THE ARMY FIELD MANUAL.

THREE DAYS LATER, THE HOUSE OF REPRESENTA-TIVES FAILED TO OVERRIDE THE VETO.

IN RESPONSE TO A REPORTING REQUIREMENT OF THE INTELLIGENCE AUTHORIZATION ACT, THE CIA STATED THAT ALL THEIR INTERROGATION TECH-NIQUES COMPLIED WITH THE LAW.

THIS WAS INACCURATE. DIAPERS, NUDITY, DIETARY MANIPULATION, AND WATER DOUSING WERE USED EXTENSIVELY AND ALL UNACCEPTABLE TO THE LAW.

ON JUNE 10, 2008, THE SSCI HELD A HEARING AFTER MEMBERS WERE GIVEN LIMITED ACCESS TO A DOJ MEMORANDUM ON THE DETENTION AND INTERROGATION PROGRAM. IN RESPONSE TO CLAIMS OF THE EFFEC-TIVENESS OF EITS BY THE COUNTERTERRORISM CENTER (CTC) LEGAL TEAM, THE COMMITTEE SUBMITTED QUESTIONS CONCERNING HOW THE CIA ASSESSED THE EFFECTIVENESS OF THE DETENTION AND INTERROGA-TION PROGRAM.

IN A RESPONSE THAT WAS NEVER SUBMITTED TO THE COMMITTEE, THE CIA ACKNOWLEDGED THAT THE CTC LEGAL TEAM HAD PROVIDED INACCURATE INFORMATION. ON OCTOBER 17, 2008, THE CIA INFORMED THE COMMITTEE THAT IT WOULD NOT RESPOND TO THE QUESTIONS. SEVERAL COMMITTEE MEMBERS REFERRED TO THIS REFUSAL TO RESPOND AS . . .

UNPRECEDENTED AND SIMPLY UNACCEPTABLE!

APPALLING!

AFTERMATH OF CIA DESTRUCTION OF INTERROGATION VIDEOS

THE COMMITTEE'S SCRUTINY OF THE CIA'S DETENTION AND INTERROGATION PROGRAM CONTINUED INTO THE 111TH CONGRESS. ON FEBRUARY 11, 2009, THE COMMITTEE HELD A BUSINESS MEETING AT WHICH THE STAFF PRESENTED A MEMO ON THE CONTENT OF CIA OPERATIONAL CABLES DEALING WITH THE INTERROGATION OF ABU ZUBAYDAH AND ABD AL-RAHIM AL-NASHIRI IN 2002.

A SMALL NUMBER OF STAFF HAD BEEN ALLOWED TO REVIEW THE CABLES AT CIA HEADQUARTERS AND HAD TESTIFIED THAT THEY PROVIDED "A MORE THAN ADEQUATE REPRESENTATION" OF WHAT WAS ON THE DESTROYED CIA INTERROGATION VIDEOTAPES.

WHEN IT WAS EVIDENT THAT THERE WERE HUGE PROBLEMS AND INCONSISTENCIES IN CIA REPRESENTATIONS AND THERE WAS A NEED TO DISCOVER WHAT WAS REALLY GOING ON, THE SSCI, ON MARCH 5, 2009, BY A VOTE OF 14-1, ELECTED TO PERFORM AN EXPANDED REVIEW OF THE CIA'S DETENTION AND INTERROGATION PROGRAM.

ON DECEMBER 13, 2012, AFTER A REVIEW OF MORE THAN 6 MILLION PAGES OF RECORDS, THE SSCI APPROVED A 6,300-PAGE STUDY OF THE CIA'S DETENTION AND INTERROGATION PROGRAM. AND ON APRIL 3, 2014, BY A BIPARTISAN VOTE OF 11-3 THEY AGREED TO SEND THE REVISED FINDINGS AND CONCLUSIONS TO THE PRESIDENT FOR DECLASSIFICATION AND PUBLIC RELEASE.

ABU ZUBAYDAH WAS RENDERED TO CIA CUSTODY IN MARCH 2002. THAT ZUBAYDAH STOPPED COOPERATING WITH DEBRIEFERS USING TRADITIONAL TECHNIQUES IS NOT SUPPORTED BY CIA RECORDS.

IN EARLY JUNE 2002, HIS INTERROGATORS SUGGESTED HE SPEND SEVERAL WEEKS IN ISOLATION. HE SPENT 47 DAYS IN ISOLATION. HE PROVIDED INFORMATION ON AL-QA'IDA ACTIVITIES, PLANS, CAPABILITIES, RELATIONS, PERSONALITIES, DECISION-MAKING PROCESSES, AND MORE, ALL BEFORE HIS ISOLATION.

AFTER ABOUT FOUR MONTHS OF INTERROGATION, ZUBAYDAH STOPPED COOPERATING AND HE SHUT DOWN . . .

NO MORE!

I WILL NOT TALK TO FBI, JUST YOU!

HE THEN WAS SUBJECTED TO EITS, INCLUDING WATERBOARDING.

HE WAS . . . EMPLOYING CLASSIC RESISTANCE . . . AND IT WAS CLEAR TO US . . . [THAT WE NEEDED] SOME SIGNIFICANT INTERVENTION.

WE WANTED IDEAS ABOUT WHAT APPROACHES MIGHT BE USEFUL TO GET INFORMATION FROM PEOPLE LIKE ABU ZUBAYDAH AND OTHER UNCOOPERATIVE DETAINEES THAT WE JUDGED WERE WITHHOLDING TIME-SENSITIVE, PERISHABLE INTELLIGENCE.

KEEP IN MIND . . . THIS WASN'T INTERROGATING A SNUFFY THAT'S PICKED UP ON THE BATTLEFIELD. THE REQUIREMENT TO BE IN THE CIA DETENTION PROGRAM IS KNOWLEDGE OF AN ATTACK AGAINST THE UNITED STATES OR ITS INTERESTS OR KNOWLEDGE OF THE LOCATION OF USAMA BIN LADEN OR AYMAN AL-ZAWAHIRI.

HE HARDLY WITHHELD INFORMATION . . .

AND AS I'VE TOLD YOU ABOUT THEIR THINKING OF THE UNITED STATES . . .

THE REPRESENTATION THAT THE "REQUIREMENT TO BE IN THE CIA DETENTION PROGRAM IS KNOWLEDGE OF AN ATTACK AGAINST THE UNITED STATES OR ITS INTERESTS OR KNOWLEDGE OF THE LOCATION OF USAMA BIN LADEN OR AYMAN AL-ZAWAHIRI" IS INCONSISTENT WITH HOW THE CIA'S DETENTION AND INTERROGATION PROGRAM OPERATED FROM ITS INCEPTION. NUMEROUS INDIVIDUALS HAD BEEN DETAINED AND SUBJECTED TO THE CIA'S EITS, DESPITE DOUBTS AND QUESTIONS SURROUNDING THEIR KNOWLEDGE OF TERRORIST THREATS AND THE LOCATION OF SENIOR AL-QA'IDA LEADERSHIP.

SO TELL ME ABOUT BIN LADEN.

WHO?

I HAVE NEVER HEARD OF HIM.

WE BEGAN IN THE SPRING OF 2002. WE HAD A VERY HIGH VALUE DETAINEE, ABU ZUBAYDAH. WE KNEW HE KNEW A LOT.

HE WOULD NOT TALK. WE WERE GOING NOWHERE WITH HIM. THE DECISION WAS MADE, WE'VE GOT TO DO SOMETHING, WE'VE GOT TO HAVE AN INTERVENTION HERE. WHAT IS IT WE CAN DO?

THE REPRESENTATION THAT ABU ZUBAYDAH "WOULD NOT TALK" IS INCONGRUENT WITH CIA RECORDS. THE CIA ASSESSMENT THAT HE KNEW A LOT REFLECTED AN INACCURATE ASSESSMENT MADE OF HIM PRIOR TO HIS CAPTURE.

PRIOR TO HIS CAPTURE, THE CIA HAD TESTIMONY FROM A SINGLE SOURCE THAT INDICATED ABU ZUBAYDAH WAS AN AL-QA'IDA LEADER. THAT TESTI-MONY WAS RETRACTED IN JULY 2002.

THE MAN'S NAME IS ABU ZUBAYDAH AND HE'S CLOSE TO BIN LADEN. MAYBE THIRD OR FOURTH FROM THE TOP.

AFTER ZUBAYDAH WAS SUBJECTED TO THE EITS, THE CHIEF OF BASE WROTE,

I DO NOT BELIEVE AZ WAS AS WIRED WITH AL-QA'IDA AS WE BELIEVED . . .

A REVIEW OF INTELLIGENCE GATHERED FROM ZUBAYDAH PRIOR TO HIM BEING SUBJECTED TO EITS REVEALED . . .

HE'S GIVEN US A TREASURE TROVE!

HOW FAR DOWN THE LINE DOES AL-QA'IDA TRAIN ITS OPERATIVES FOR INTERROGATION RESISTANCE?

IT'S RATHER BROADLY BASED.

VICE CHAIRMAN BOND

SO EVEN IF YOU CAPTURED THE AL-QA'IDA FACILITATOR, PROBABLY THE ARMY FIELD MANUAL STUFF ARE THINGS THAT HE'S ALREADY BEEN TRAINED ON, AND HE KNOWS THAT HE DOESN'T HAVE TO TALK.

WE WOULD EXPECT THAT, YES, SENATOR.

DIRECTOR HAYDEN

A REVIEW OF CIA RECORDS ON THIS TOPIC IDENTIFIED NO RECORDS TO INDICATE THAT AL-QA'IDA HAD CONDUCTED "BROADLY BASED" INTERROGATION RESISTANCE TRAINING. THE CIA REPEATEDLY REPRESENTED THAT ABU ZUBAYDAH "WROTE AL-QA'IDA'S MANUAL ON RESISTANCE TECHNIQUES."

NOW WHAT SHOULD I WRITE NEXT?

CIA RECORDS DO NOT SUPPORT THE CLAIM THAT ZUBAYDAH WROTE AN INTERROGATION RESISTANCE TRAINING MANUAL.

WHEN ASKED ABOUT INTERROGATION RESISTANCE ZUBAYDAH STATED "BOTH KHALDAN CAMP AND FARUQ CAMP AT LEAST PERIODICALLY INCLUDED INSTRUCTION IN HOW TO MANAGE CAPTIVITY."

HE EXPLAINED THAT HE INFORMED TRAINEES AT THE TRAINING CAMP THAT "NO BROTHER SHOULD BE EXPECTED TO HOLD OUT FOR AN EXTENDED TIME." AND THAT CAPTURED INDIVIDUALS WILL PROVIDE INFORMATION IN DETENTION. FOR THAT REASON, THE CAPTURED INDIVIDUALS SHOULD "EXPECT THAT THE ORGANIZATION WILL MAKE ADJUSTMENTS TO PROTECT PEOPLE AND PLANS WHEN SOMEONE WITH KNOWLEDGE IS CAPTURED."

ALL THOSE INVOLVED IN THE QUESTIONING OF DETAINEES HAVE BEEN CAREFULLY CHOSEN AND CAREFULLY SCREENED. ONCE THEY ARE SELECTED, THEY MUST COMPLETE MORE THAN 250 HOURS OF SPECIALIZED TRAINING . . . BEFORE THEY ARE ALLOWED TO COME FACE-TO-FACE WITH A TERRORIST.

AND WE REQUIRE ADDITIONAL FIELDWORK UNDER THE DIRECT SUPERVISION OF AN EXPERIENCED OFFICER BEFORE A NEW INTERROGATOR CAN DIRECT AN INTERROGATION.

THE ARMY FIELD MANUAL WAS ALSO WRITTEN TO GUIDE THE CONDUCT OF A MUCH LARGER, MUCH YOUNGER FORCE THAT TRAINS PRIMARILY TO DETAIN LARGE NUMBERS OF ENEMY PRISONERS OF WAR. THAT'S NOT WHAT THE CIA PROGRAM IS.

THE ARMY FIELD MANUAL HAS GOT TO BE DONE BY HUNDREDS AND HUNDREDS OF TEENAGERS IN BATTLEFIELD TACTICAL SITUATIONS.

WITHOUT THE BENEFIT OF A TENTH OF THE TRAINING OF YOUR PROFESSIONALS.

EXACTLY.

THE CIA TESTIMONY IS INCONGRUENT WITH INTERNAL CIA RECORDS AND THE OPERATIONAL HISTORY OF THE PROGRAM. CONTRARY TO CIA DIRECTOR MICHAEL HAYDEN'S COMMENTS AND STATEMENT FOR THE RECORD, "ALL THOSE INVOLVED IN THE QUESTIONING OF DETAINEES ARE CAREFULLY CHOSEN AND SCREENED FOR . . . PROFESSIONAL JUDGMENT AND MATURITY," CIA RECORDS SUGGEST THAT NO VETTING TOOK PLACE. INSTEAD THE COMMITTEE IDENTIFIED A NUMBER OF PERSONNEL WHOSE BACKGROUNDS INCLUDE NOTABLE DEROGATORY INFORMATION THAT CALLED INTO QUESTION THEIR ELIGIBILITY FOR EMPLOYMENT, THEIR ACCESS TO CLASSIFIED INFORMATION, AND THEIR PARTICIPATION IN CIA INTERROGATION ACTIVITIES. IN NEARLY ALL CASES, THE INFORMATION WAS KNOWN TO THE CIA PRIOR TO THEIR ASSIGNMENTS. THIS GROUP INCLUDED INDIVIDUALS WHO, AMONG OTHER ISSUES, HAD ENGAGED IN INAPPROPRIATE DETAINEE INTERROGATIONS, HAD WORKPLACE ANGER ISSUES, AND HAD REPORTEDLY ADMITTED TO SEXUAL ASSAULT.

DIRECTOR HAYDEN'S TESTIMONY ON THE REQUIRED HOURS OF TRAINING FOR CIA INTER-ROGATORS IS INCONSISTENT WITH THE EARLY HISTORY OF THE PROGRAM. RECORDS INDICATE THAT CIA OFFICERS AND CONTRACTORS IN 2002 DID NOT UNDERGO ANY INTERROGATION TRAINING. THE INITIAL TRAINING WAS DESIGNED AND CONDUCTED BY AN AGENT WHO HAD NEVER BEEN TRAINED IN OR CONDUCTED INTERROGATIONS AND WHO HAD BEEN SANC-TIONED FOR USING ABUSIVE INTERROGATION TECHNIQUES.

ALL INTERROGATION SESSIONS . . . HAVE TO BE OBSERVED BY NON-PARTICIPANTS TO ENSURE THE PROCEDURES ARE APPLIED APPROPRIATELY AND SAFELY. ANY OBSERVER CAN CALL "KNOCK IT OFF" AT ANY TIME. THEY ARE AUTHORIZED TO TERMINATE AN INTERROGATION IMMEDIATELY.

THE TESTIMONY IS INCONGRUENT WITH CIA RECORDS. DURING THE INTERROGATION OF ABU ZUBAYDAH, CIA PERSONNEL OBJECTED TO THE USE OF THE ENHANCED TECHNIQUES, STATING THAT IT WAS "HIGHLY UNLIKELY" HE POSSESSED THE THREAT INFORMATION THEY WERE SEEKING. THEY SAID THE PRESSURES APPLIED TO ZUBAYDAH APPROACHED "THE LEGAL LIMIT."

DIRECTOR HAYDEN

EVERYBODY WATCHING HAS--EVERY INDIVIDUAL HAS AN ABSOLUTE RIGHT TO STOP THE PROCEDURE BY SIMPLY SAYING, "STOP!"

LET'S GET ON WITH THIS. AND LET'S REFRAIN FROM USING SPECULATIVE LANGUAGE AS TO THE LEGALITY OF GIVEN ACTIVITIES.

DID IT HAPPEN? IT'S NEVER HAPPENED?

DURING THE KSM INTERROGATION SESSIONS ON MARCH 13, 2003, PRIOR TO KSM'S THIRD WATERBOARD SESSION, THE ON-SITE MEDICAL OFFICER RAISED CONCERNS THAT THE SESSION WOULD EXCEED THE LIMITS OF GUIDELINES FOR THE WATERBOARD. THE SESSION CONTINUED AFTER APPROVAL FROM AN ATTORNEY AT CIA HEADQUARTERS. THE MEDICAL OFFICER WOULD LATER WRITE, "THINGS ARE SLOWLY EVOLVING FROM MEDICAL OFFICERS BEING VIEWED AS THE . . . LIMITING FACTOR TO . . . KEEPING EVERY-ONE'S BUTT OUT OF TROUBLE." AS WAS THE CASE WITH SEVERAL OTHER CIA DETAINEES, ABD AL-RAHIM AL-NASHIRI WAS REPEATEDLY SUBJECTED TO THE CIA'S ENHANCED INTERROGATION TECHNIQUES AT THE DIRECTION OF CIA HEADQUARTERS DESPITE . . .

NO, WE'RE NOT AWARE . . . [CIA GENERAL COUNSEL] JOHN RIZZO . . . POINTED OUT IT'S JUST NOT THE ABILITY TO STOP IT, IT IS AN OBLIGATION TO STOP IT IF THEY BELIEVE SOMETHING IS HAPPENING THAT IS UNAUTHORIZED.

I THINK HE'S HAD ENOUGH!

KNOCK IT OFF!

AND I AGREE.

OPPOSITION FROM CIA INTERROGATORS.

DID ANY CIA PERSONNEL EXPRESS RESERVATIONS ABOUT BEING ENGAGED IN THE INTERROGATION OR THESE TECHNIQUES THAT WERE USED?

I'M NOT AWARE OF ANY. THESE GUYS ARE MORE EXPERIENCED. NO.

ANY DEVIATIONS FROM APPROVED PROCEDURES AND PRACTICES THAT ARE SEEN ARE TO BE IMMEDIATELY REPORTED AND IMMEDIATE CORRECTIVE ACTION TAKEN, INCLUDING REFERRING TO THE CIA OFFICE OF INSPECTOR GENERAL AND TO THE DEPARTMENT OF JUSTICE, AS APPROPRIATE.

THIS STATEMENT IS INCONGRUENT WITH CIA RECORDS. FOR EXAMPLE, FROM AUGUST 4 TO 23, 2002, THE CIA SUBJECTED ABU ZUBAYDAH TO ITS ENHANCED TECHNIQUES ON A NEAR 24-HOUR-PER-DAY BASIS. THIS WAS DISTURBING TO CIA PERSONNEL, AND THEY OBJECTED TO CIA HEADQUARTERS.

SO WHAT'S THE ANSWER?

THEY ORDER US TO CONTINUE.

MULTIPLE INDIVIDUALS INVOLVED IN THE INTERROGATION OF CIA DETAINEE ABD AL-RAHIM AL-NASHIRI FAILED TO REPORT INAPPROPRIATE ACTIVITY REGARDING THE USE OF A HANDGUN AND POWER TOOL TO THREATEN AL-NASHIRI.

LOOK, I NEVER RECEIVED GUIDANCE ON HOW TO REPORT THIS

AND I'M NOT SURE IT'S SOMETHING I SHOULD REPORT.

IN ADDITION, CIA RECORDS INDICATE THAT AT LEAST 17 DETAINEES WERE SUBJECTED TO THE ENHANCED TECHNIQUES FOR WHICH THEY WERE NOT APPROVED.

THE ARMY FIELD MANUAL IS DESIGNED FOR THE FOLKS AT GUANTANAMO TO INTERROGATE A RIFLEMAN THAT WAS IN THE EMPLOY OF GULBUDDIN HEKMATYAR. THAT GUY NEVER GETS INTO OUR PROGRAM. THE TICKET INTO THIS PROGRAM IS KNOWLEDGE OF THREAT TO THE HOMELAND OR THE INTERESTS OF THE UNITED STATES OR KNOWLEDGE OF LOCATION 1 OR 2.

THIS TESTIMONY IS INCONGRUENT WITH CIA DETENTION AND INTERROGATION RECORDS. FOR EXAMPLE, NUMEROUS INDIVIDUALS HAVE BEEN DETAINED AND SUBJECTED TO ENHANCED TECHNIQUES DESPITE DOUBTS AND QUESTIONS SURROUNDING THEIR KNOWLEDGE OF TERRORIST THREATS AND THE LOCATION OF AL-QA'IDA LEADERSHIP. THEY INCLUDE: ASADULLAH, ABU HUDHAIFA, ARSALA KHAN, JANAT GUL, SHARIF AL-MASRI, SAYYID IBRAHIM, AND MANY MORE.

CIA REPRESENTATIONS SUGGESTING THAT EVERY CIA DETAINEE PROVIDED INTELLIGENCE REPORTING ARE NOT SUPPORTED BY CIA RECORDS. CIA RECORDS INDICATE THAT 34% OF ALL CIA DETAINEES PROVIDED NO INTELLIGENCE AND NEARLY 70% PRODUCED FEWER THAN 15 INTELLIGENCE REPORTS. OF THE 39 DETAINEES WHO, ACCORDING TO THE CIA, WERE SUBJECTED TO ENHANCED INTERROGATION, NEARLY 20% PRODUCED NO INTELLIGENCE REPORTS, WHILE 40% PRODUCED FEWER THAN 15 INTELLIGENCE REPORTS.

THE CHRONOLOGY PROVIDED IN THIS TESTIMONY IS INACCURATE. PRIOR TO KSM'S CAPTURE, COVERAGE OF A KNOWN AL-QA'IDA E-MAIL ACCOUNT REVEALED . . .

SINCE WE BEGAN THIS IN THE SUMMER OF 2002, THE 97 DETAINEES HAVE HELPED US BY THEIR TESTIMONY CREATE 8,000 INTELLIGENCE REPORTS.

DIRECTOR HAYDEN

OF THE 8,000 REPORTS THAT WERE PROVIDED, AS YOU SAID, BY 30 OF THE DETAINEES--

BY ALL 97, MA'AM.

MARCH 2003, KSM GIVES US INFORMATION ABOUT AN AL-QA'IDA OPERATIVE, MAJID KHAN . . . KSM WAS AWARE THAT MAJID HAD BEEN RECENTLY CAPTURED. KSM, POSSIBLY BELIEVING THAT KHAN WAS TALKING, ADMITTED TO HAVING TASKED MAJID WITH DELIVERING $50,000 TO SOME OF HAMBALI'S OPERATIVES IN DECEMBER 2002 . . . SO NOW WE GO TO KHAN, AND WE TELL HIM, HEY, YOUR UNCLE JUST TOLD US ABOUT THE MONEY. HE ACKNOWLEDGED THAT HE DELIVERED THE MONEY TO AN OPERATIVE NAMED ZUBAIR. HE PROVIDED ZUBAIR'S PHYSICAL DESCRIPTION AND PHONE NUMBER. BASED ON THAT WE CAPTURED ZUBAIR IN JUNE.

LOOK AT THIS E-MAIL! A GUY FROM BALTIMORE NAMED MAJID KHAN . . .

GOT IT! HE WENT TO BANGKOK AND GOT INVOLVED WITH SOMEONE NAMED ZUBAIR!

THIS LED TO THE CAPTURE OF MAJID KHAN AND SUBSEQUENTLY TO THE CAPTURE OF ZUBAIR. HIS CAPTURE HAD NOTHING TO DO WITH CIA DETAINEE REPORTING.

DIRECTOR HAYDEN

WORKING WITH AN ENTITY OF A FOREIGN GOVERNMENT, WE USED THAT INFORMATION TO CAPTURE ANOTHER HAMBALI LIEUTENANT, A FELLOW NAMED LILLIE--WHO IS ALSO ON YOUR LIST OF CIA DETAINEES--WHO PROVIDED THE LOCATION OF HAMBALI. AND THAT LOCATION INFORMATION LED US TO HIS CAPTURE.

IN AN OPERATION THAT INCLUDED SURVEILLANCE OF A BUSINESS Q, HAMBALI ASSOCIATE AMER WAS IMMEDIATELY COOPERATIVE AND ASSISTED IN THE ARREST OF LILLIE HOURS LATER AT APPROXIMATELY 6:00 PM.

DURING HIS ARREST, LILLIE WAS FOUND TO HAVE A KEY FOB IN HIS POSSESSION IMPRINTED WITH AN ADDRESS OF AN APARTMENT BUILDING IN AYUTTHAYA, THAILAND. IN RESPONSE TO QUESTIONING, WITHIN MINUTES OF CAPTURE, LILLIE ADMITTED . . .

VERY WELL . . . THAT ADDRESS IS WHERE HAMBALI IS STAYING!

HOURS LATER . . .

YOU'RE UNDER ARREST, SIR!

ACCORDING TO THE CHIEF OF THE CTC'S SOUTHEAST ASIA BRANCH, "THE CIA STUMBLED ONTO HAMBALI . . . IT WASN'T POLICE WORK, IT WASN'T GOOD TARGETING, . . . WE STUMBLED OVER IT AND IT YIELDED UP HAMBALI."

DIRECTOR HAYDEN

THIS PROPOSED PROGRAM YOU HAVE IN FRONT OF YOU HAS BEEN INFORMED BY OUR EXPERIENCE AND . . . BY THE COMMENTS OF OUR DETAINEES. IT'S BUILT ON THE PARTICULAR PSYCHOLOGICAL PROFILE OF THE PEOPLE WE HAVE AND EXPECT TO GET--AL-QA'IDA OPERATIVES. PERCEIVING THEMSELVES TO BE TRUE BELIEVERS IN A RELIGIOUS WAR, DETAINEES BELIEVE THEY ARE MORALLY BOUND TO RESIST UNTIL ALLAH HAS SENT THEM A BURDEN TOO GREAT FOR THEM TO WITHSTAND. AT THAT POINT--AND THAT POINT VARIES BY DETAINEE--THEIR COOPERATION IN THEIR OWN HEART AND SOUL BECOMES BLAMELESS AND THEY ENTER INTO THIS COOPERATIVE RELATIONSHIP WITH OUR DEBRIEFERS.

I THINK HE'S READY.

MANY ASSERTIONS REGARDING PHYSICAL OR THREATENED ABUSE ARE EGREGIOUS AND ARE SIMPLY NOT TRUE. ON THEIR FACE, THEY AREN'T EVEN CREDIBLE. THREATS OF ACTS OF SODOMY, THE ARREST AND RAPE OF FAMILY MEMBERS, THE INTENTIONAL INFECTION OF HIV OR ANY OTHER DISEASE HAVE NEVER BEEN AND WOULD NEVER BE AUTHORIZED.

CIA RECORDS DO NOT INDICATE THAT CIA DETAINEES DESCRIBED A RELIGIOUS BASIS FOR COOPERATING IN ASSOCIATION WITH THE CIA'S ENHANCED INTERROGATION TECHNIQUES. THE CIA HAS REFERRED ONLY TO ABU ZUBAYDAH IN THE CONTEXT OF THIS REPRESENTATION.

ON MAY 14, 2002, MORE THAN TWO MONTHS PRIOR TO HIS BEING GIVEN THE ENHANCED TECHNIQUES, HE TOLD INVESTIGATORS . . .

IF I POSSESSED ANY MORE INFORMATION ON FUTURE THREATS, I WOULD SHARE IT WITH YOU.

THE SHARIA GIVES ME PERMISSION IN MY CURRENT SITUATION.

A WEEK LATER, HE TOLD US . . .

I HAVE PRAYED MY ISTIKHARAH (SEEKING GOD'S GUIDANCE) AND AM NOW WILLING TO TELL WHAT I REALLY KNOW.

THIS TESTIMONY IS INCONGRUENT WITH CIA INTERROGATION RECORDS.

AS DOCUMENTED IN MAY 2004, CIA INTERROGATORS THREATENED ABD AL-RAHIM AL-NASHIRI, KSM, AND ZUBAYDAH WITH . . .

COME CLEAN OR EVEN YOUR *FAMILY* WON'T BE SAFE!

RECTAL EXAMS WERE STANDARD OPERATING PROCEDURE. AT LEAST FIVE DETAINEES WERE SUBJECTED TO RECTAL REHYDRATION OR RECTAL FEEDING.

DIRECTOR HAYDEN

THE ALLEGATION IN THE REPORT THAT A CIA MEDICAL OFFICER THREATENED A DETAINEE, STATING THAT MEDICAL CARE WAS CONDITIONAL ON COOPERATION IS BLATANTLY FALSE. HEALTH CARE HAS ALWAYS BEEN ADMINISTERED BASED UPON DETAINEE'S NEEDS.

HAS THERE BEEN ANY USE OF ANY KIND OF DRUGS OR WITHHOLDING OF ANY KIND OF DRUGS OR MEDICATION?

NO, ABSOLUTELY NOT.

SO THIS IS NOT TIPPING THE BOARD AND PUTTING HIS HEAD UNDERNEATH THE WATER?

NO. IT'S SLIGHTLY INCLINED, CLOTH, POURING OF WATER UNDER THE RULES I JUST LAID OUT, SENATOR.

THIS TESTIMONY IS INCONGRUENT WITH CIA RECORDS. FOR EXAMPLE, AS CIA INTERROGATORS PREPARED FOR THE AUGUST 2002 "ENHANCED INTERROGATION" PHASE OF ABU ZUBAYDAH'S INTERROGATION . . .

HEADQUARTERS HAS JUST INFORMED US THAT THE INTERROGATION PROCESS WILL TAKE PRECEDENCE OVER PREVENTING ZUBAYDAH'S WOUNDS FROM BECOMING INFECTED.

CIA DETAINEES ABU HAZIM AND ABD AL-KARIM EACH BROKE A FOOT TRYING TO ESCAPE CAPTURE AND WERE PLACED IN CASTS. DESPITE THEIR MEDICAL PROBLEMS, THEY FACED REPEATED WALLINGS AND STANDING SLEEP DEPRIVATION. AL-KARIM WOULD HAVE ARTHRITIS AND LIMITATION OF MOTION FOR THE REST OF HIS LIFE.

THE TESTIMONY IS INCONGRUENT WITH CIA INTERROGATION RECORDS. THE WATERBOARDING OF KSM INVOLVED INTERROGATORS USING THEIR HANDS TO MAINTAIN A ONE-INCH "POOL" OF WATER OVER KSM'S NOSE AND MOUTH IN AN EFFORT TO MAKE IT IMPOSSIBLE TO INGEST ALL THE WATER BEING POURED ON HIM. ACCORDING TO THE ATTENDING MEDICAL OFFICER, IT BECAME A "SERIES OF NEAR DROWNINGS."

THIS TESTIMONY IS INCONGRUENT WITH CIA INTERROGATION RECORDS. THESE INDICATE THAT CIA DETAINEES SUFFERED PHYSICAL INJURIES BEYOND BRUISING FROM SHACKLING AS WELL AS PSYCHOLOGICAL PROBLEMS.

DURING A WATERBOARD SESSION, ABU ZUBAYDAH "BECAME COMPLETELY UNRESPONSIVE, WITH BUBBLES RISING THROUGH HIS OPEN, FULL MOUTH" AND ONLY REGAINED CONSCIOUSNESS AFTER RECEIVING A "XYPHOID THRUST."

DURING THE APPLICATION OF THE CIA'S ENHANCED INTERROGATION TECHNIQUES, KSM WAS DESCRIBED AS "TIRED AND SORE," WITH ABRASIONS ON HIS ANKLES, SHINS, AND WRISTS, AS WELL AS ON THE BACK OF HIS HEAD.

AND AT CIA **DETENTION SITE COBALT**, INTERROGATORS USED "ROUGH TAKEDOWNS," DESCRIBED AS TAKING A NAKED DETAINEE OUTSIDE OF THE CELL, PLACING A HOOD OVER HIS HEAD, AND DRAGGING HIM UP AND DOWN A LONG CORRIDOR.

THE MOST SERIOUS INJURY THAT I'M AWARE OF--AND I'LL ASK THE EXPERTS TO ADD ANY COLOR THEY WANT, SENATOR--IS BRUISING AS A RESULT OF SHACKLING.

DID ANYBODY DIE?

NO.

NOT ONE PERSON?

NO ONE.

THE COMMITTEE IS AWARE THAT THERE IS A LONE INDIVIDUAL WHO DIED IN CIA CUSTODY PRIOR TO THE INITIATION OF THE PROGRAM.

PRIOR TO THE INITIATION OF WHAT?

THIS PROGRAM. IN FACT, THE DISCIPLINE OF THIS PROGRAM IS A PRODUCT OF OR RESULT OF THE UNDISCIPLINED ACTIVITY THAT TOOK PLACE EARLIER.

GUL RAHMAN WAS NOT PART OF THIS PROGRAM, BUT I UNDERSTAND IT WAS IN CIA CUSTODY.

THIS TESTIMONY IS INCONGRUENT WITH CIA RECORDS.

GUL RAHMAN DIED IN CIA CUSTODY AT THE CIA'S **DETENTION SITE COBALT**, AFTER BEING RENDERED THERE IN NOVEMBER 2002. AT THE TIME, **DETENTION SITE COBALT** WAS DESCRIBED AS A PLACE WHERE THE CIA COULD DETAIN SUSPECTED TERRORISTS FOR THE PURPOSE OF "INTENSE INTERROGATION" BY CIA OFFICERS. DDO JAMES PAVITT TOLD THE INSPECTOR GENERAL THAT "THERE WERE SOME WHO SAY THAT [COBALT] IS NOT A CIA FACILITY, BUT THAT IS 'BULLSHIT.'"

CIA RECORDS REVEAL THAT RAHMAN WAS SUBJECTED TO . . .

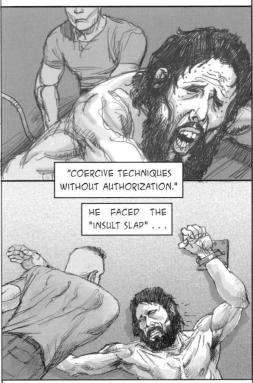

"COERCIVE TECHNIQUES WITHOUT AUTHORIZATION."

HE FACED THE "INSULT SLAP" . . .

AND THEN, NUDE ON THE LOWER HALF OF HIS BODY, HE WAS SHACKLED TO THE WALL OF HIS CELL IN A SHORT CHAIN POSITION REQUIRING HIM TO SIT ON THE BARE CONCRETE FLOOR.

SOMETIME LATER HE DIED.

AFTERWORD
SCOTT HORTON

WHEN, ON DECEMBER 9, 2014, the Senate Select Committee on Intelligence released its torture report—or, more accurately, a redaction-studded version of the report's executive summary—it delivered far more than the title promised. This was no bureaucratic whitewash. It avoided the tepid style of most congressional documents, opting instead for a clinical, precise, and engaging narrative that patiently unfolds one of the most dysfunctional and embarrassing episodes in the history of American spycraft. This graphic edition crisply summarizes and dramatically visualizes this report.

The CIA that emerges from these pages bears almost no resemblance to the modest organization created at the end of World War II. It has an annual budget of more than $50 billion, as well as its own private army, and with its state-of-the-art drones equipped with missiles, its own air force. It wages wars in Pakistan, Yemen, Somalia, and across the nations of the African Sahel, and it also mobilizes proxy armies to do its bidding—arming Afghan warlords to topple the Taliban in 2002, seconding the Ethiopian military for an invasion of Somalia in 2006, and recruiting African tribesmen to battle Moammar Qaddafi in 2011. The agency also operates a far-flung assassination program, deploying drones, bombs, bullets, and other weapons to kill hundreds of individuals who pose some perceived threat, with no pretense of recourse to the judicial system.

This report can be read as a deep exploration of a horribly failed CIA program of the war on terror era. However, its broader significance is as a mapping exercise. It shows us the essence of the relationship that has developed between the CIA and the other essential Washington powerholders: the White House, Pentagon, State Department, Justice Department, Congress (and particularly its oversight organs that in theory keep an eye on the CIA), the courts, and the media. What it reveals is an institution that is widely feared and that few are willing to question or challenge. Never has the CIA been as powerful, as wealthy, and as unaccountable as the institution portrayed in this report.

* * *

The authors of the program recognized almost immediately that it violated both domestic American law and such international treaties as the Geneva Conventions, the U.N. Convention Against Torture, and the International Covenant on Civil and Political Rights. The report reveals that these architects were from the outset pre-occupied with the real risk of criminal prosecution. This led them to enlist a handful of carefully selected lawyers who could be counted upon to offer opinions that the program was lawful and that the techniques were not torture. Having obtained the requisite fig leaf from the Department of Justice, which guaranteed that no criminal charges could be brought, the authors of the program then won the official approval of the National Security Council, chaired by none other than President George W. Bush.

This was a key point. Although American forces had used some of these torture techniques for nearly a century, starting with the Philippine counterinsurgency campaign (1899–1902), they were officially forbidden. The Bush decision represented the first and only time in American history that the executive authority at its highest level had put its stamp of approval on practices that the United States itself had previously classified as torture.

While the black sites and torture techniques were banned by Barack Obama in one of his first official acts as president, the report discloses that the program faced strong internal opposition even under his predecessor. Indeed, some of the most hellish components were terminated on the apparent initiative of President Bush himself in the fall of 2006, more than two years before the transition to the new administration. Similarly, in the process of packing up before departing Washington, the Bush administration systematically rescinded almost all of its torture-friendly legal opinions, recognizing that they had been widely ridiculed and were no longer tenable.

Not surprisingly, Dick Cheney emerges in the report as the *fons et origio* of the program, and its last, uncompromising defender. Cheney had no legal standing to approve the program—he appears to have invoked the authority of the president without actually involving him.[1] He also intervened personally and repeatedly to defend his brainchild against internal critics, including the CIA's Inspector General, John Helgerson. Cheney demanded complete impunity for those who worked in the program; in his view, not even the torture and murder of an entirely innocent person—such as Gul Rahman, who was allowed to freeze to death in a CIA holding pen north of Kabul known as the Salt Pit—merited punishment of any sort. The interrogators were not criminals but patriots, seeking to avert another round of terrorist mayhem.

Still, not all the blame can be laid at Cheney's door. The DOJ, too, has some explaining to do, although it initially rebuffed the agency's quest for legal cover. The CIA's lawyers, led by general counsel John Rizzo and the lead attorney for the National Counterterrorism Center, Robert Eatinger, first lobbied for a "declination letter"—a pledge not to prosecute certain criminal acts before they have been committed. This was refused on the grounds that the DOJ could not openly appear to license criminal acts. Only then did Rizzo and Eatinger attempt to demonstrate that the torture techniques were not, in fact, torture. This opinion the DOJ was willing to confirm, in a remarkably credulous fashion, without making any attempt to verify the facts—many of which turned out to be false.

Following the election of Barack Obama, the new attorney general, Eric Holder, resurrected the traditional view that waterboarding and several of the other techniques constituted torture and were prohibited by law. However, the Obama DOJ continued to implement its predecessor's playbook, immunizing all of the participants in the torture program. The only person actually prosecuted was a CIA agent, John Kiriakou, who had been audacious enough to reveal the White House's stamp of approval on the program, as well as identifying two fellow agents linked to abuses.

True, a special prosecutor named John Durham was appointed to investigate the most serious allegations of torture and abuse, including three cases of homicide clearly connected to CIA interrogations. But Durham was instructed that the accused agents could rely on the Bush-era DOJ opinions, now rescinded, that had legitimized waterboarding and other horrific techniques. The report strongly suggests that Durham's investigation was merely the final phase of an elaborate exercise in damage control. In these pages, the DOJ resembles nothing so much as the CIA's personal attorney, engaged not in law enforcement but in criminal defense work.

* * *

And what of the Department of State? The diplomatic and consular corps historically provide support to intelligence agents, and also tend to view them with some measure of disdain. Indeed, the rivalry between the CIA and State Department has been acute since 1947, when the intelligence agency was launched with the informal motto "Bigger than State by [19]48." (The CIA's budget in fact exceeded that of the State Department in 1948, and in every year since).

The report reveals a relationship between Langley and Foggy Bottom that is by any measure humiliating to the diplomats. They are lied to at almost every turn. It is understood that State Department officials, and particularly Secretary Colin Powell, cannot be trusted with sensitive information about the program because they did not and would not support it. At one point, the report quotes an internal CIA e-mail to the effect that "Powell would blow his stack if he were to be briefed on what's been going on."[2] Meanwhile, Powell and his staffers were repeatedly herded onto the public stage to spread the agency's lies, and to suffer embarrassment when they were exposed.

The CIA treated Congress with little more respect, even though the legislature appropriates funds for the CIA, makes the laws that govern its conduct, and has the power of oversight and investigation into its activities. Among other things, the agency is required to brief senior congressional leaders on its covert programs. The report concludes that while some of these briefings did occur, the CIA systematically downplayed the extent and brutality of its interrogation program—and when further details were requested by the congressional leadership, it tried its best to (in the words of one internal e-mail) "get . . . off the hook on the cheap."[3] Of course the easiest way to deal with these requests was to ignore them entirely, which is often what happened.

At the same time, the report indicates a real failure of oversight—and of political will—by the Congress. Its investigation was undertaken only after the program had been brought to its end, when a senior CIA officer was acknowledged to have destroyed key evidence of waterboarding. There was no effort to pursue questions while the program was actually in effect. Moreover, the entire protracted history of the Senate committee's dealings with the CIA, which ultimately led to the issuance of this report, reflects that time and again, the legislators were outmaneuvered by the agency. Congress was no match for the CIA's intrigues within the Washington Beltway.

Of course that other great public watchdog, the American press, was no more vigilant. Langley made extensive efforts to propagandize the public through both entertainment and news outlets. The fingerprints of various CIA public affairs officers could be found not only on movies like *Zero Dark Thirty* but on Fox's popular series *24*, whose very theme music intoned the ticking of a bomb. In all of these cases, torture was portrayed as something noble and necessary, and accounts were circulated to suggest that terrorist plots had been stopped in the nick of time thanks to "enhanced interrogation techniques." (Unfortunately for the CIA, this turned out to be a translation of the same euphemism used by the Gestapo: *verschärfte Vernehmung*.)

Other efforts targeted news outlets. The report finds evidence of this extensive propagandizing campaign in internal CIA communications. There is, for example, the pleading of Doug Jehl, then a prominent *New York Times* reporter (and now a foreign editor at the *Washington Post*), who apparently promised to show the interrogation techniques in the best and most favorable light—if only the CIA would leak him further information. (The agency clearly felt itself on the winning end of such bargains: when Jehl was assembling an article on the torture of Abu Zubaydah, which included forced nudity, frigid temperatures, and the threatening presence of a crudely built coffin, a CIA officer noted that "this is not necessarily an unflattering story.")[4] For CIA lawyers, of course, this flagrant hypocrisy—shoveling fake and self-serving "leaks" to friendly journalists while insisting that the courts block any disclosures in the name of national security—created a huge dilemma. What would happen if the courts learned about this double-dealing? Well, now they have. It remains to be seen what consequences, if any, this will have for the CIA's edifice of secrecy.

* * *

The report spotlights a perpetual struggle in U.S. politics, between the commitment to transparency as the fundamental basis of democratic life and the use of secrecy by the intelligence services governed by raisons d'état. As Tocqueville observed in the early nineteenth century, American citizens "luxuriate in publicity" and often amused themselves by forcing the private misdeeds of politicians and institutions into public view—subjecting them to intense and often merciless ridicule. Following in this tradition, modern congressional oversight often adopts a skeptical view of claims of secrecy, particularly when the secrecy appears to obscure mistakes, incompetence, corruption, or, as in this case, criminality.

Senator Dianne Feinstein and her colleagues agreed at the outset that they would investigate only the CIA's black site and interrogation programs. The idea was to inform the public, and to begin an essential conversation about future intelligence operations, without necessarily offering any more far-ranging conclusions. Still, in the first section of its executive summary, the report does include twenty powerful findings, most of them damning in the extreme. The CIA is roasted for its mendacity and incompetence, some of it rising far beyond the Keystone Kops level we have come to expect. (A single, amazing fact: the agency hired two unqualified psychologists to design and manage the program, paying them $80 million on a $181 million contract before it was terminated.) It failed to extract actionable intelligence with its brutal techniques while pretending exactly the opposite. Last but not least, its programs "caused immeasurable damage to the United States' public standing, as well as to the United States' longstanding global leadership on human rights in general and the prevention of torture in particular."[5]

Yet these conclusions mask others, which are suggested deep in the text of the report. One of the most important questions about the decision to introduce waterboarding and other forms of torture is simply, why? The mantra adopted by the Bush administration was that of the ticking time bomb. If the imminent explosion might cost the lives of thousands of innocents, shouldn't the state use every tool at its disposal to disarm that bomb? Yet in case after case studied by the Senate, no sense of urgency can be found. Prisoners are often locked up for weeks before they are even questioned; on other occasions, the techniques are used long after any time-sensitive information might reasonably be secured. Moreover, the report concludes that the CIA failed to perform the usual psychological tests applied to prison guards, accepting numerous candidates with violent or sadistic impulses. In many instances, then, prisoners appear to have been tortured for purely vindictive motives.

Which isn't to say that the Bush administration had no rationale at all. In footnote 857, we learn of one of the very first instances that enhanced interrogation techniques were used, on a prisoner known as Ibn al-Shaykh al-Libi.[6] While being tortured in a detention facility run for the CIA by Egyptian intelligence, al-Libi claimed that Saddam Hussein had ongoing relations with al-Qa'ida. Once the Egyptians turned al-Libi over to the CIA, he immediately recanted these claims. Nevertheless, the CIA provided his earlier, coerced statements to Colin Powell—who would use them to justify the invasion of Iraq before the United Nations Security Council—without telling Powell that the claims had been recanted and were never credible in the first place.[7] Did the Bush administration use torture specifically to secure false statements from prisoners, which could then be used for propaganda purposes? The al-Libi case certainly suggests so.

* * *

No wonder the CIA worked assiduously to keep this report from seeing the light of day. In a now famous speech delivered in March 2014 on the Senate floor, Dianne Feinstein described the many obstructive, foot-dragging techniques used by the agency. The CIA insisted that every document be reviewed internally before it was handed over to the Senate, hiring outside contractors to accomplish this supposedly secretive task. It ensured that the review of documents took place in the CIA offices, on CIA computers, which meant the agency could easily access the Senate's investigation later on. It asked the DOJ to launch a criminal investigation against Senate staffers, and demanded that the report be crammed with puzzling, sometimes reader-proof redactions.

It is unsurprising that the CIA would resort to these tactics. Some of them are precisely the sort of techniques that skilled bureaucrats have employed for decades in Washington to thwart, or at least slow down, congressional investigations, while others are espionage tricks the agency had long been trained to turn on the nation's enemies. No doubt many of the staffers involved also believed the struggle was a desperate one. Disclosure of the truth would do immense harm to the reputation of the CIA as an institution. More to the point, it was likely to do serious damage to the careers of the senior personnel who ran the torture and black sites program, many of whom had risen to the top ranks. Robert Eatinger, for example, had been a senior staff lawyer for the CIA when he first discussed the idea of a declination letter with the DOJ. Now he was the agency's acting general counsel, and he used all the powers at his command to quash the report, in which his name appeared some 1,600 times.

To the same end, the agency played a formidable backroom game. Within the White House, CIA director John Brennan patiently lobbied President Obama against the Senate report, explaining that its release would demoralize the organization and harm the careers of diligent, loyal operatives like Eatinger. It might also destroy the ability of the CIA to draw on the support of key collaborators—meaning the governments of Egypt, Lithuania, Morocco, Poland, Romania, and the

United Kingdom, which expected their involvement in the program to be kept secret. Brennan enlisted Obama's chief of staff, Denis McDonough, who offered to represent the president in brokering a final agreement between the CIA and the senators on material to be censored in the report. As it happened, McDonough proved an aggressive advocate for the CIA rather than a mediator of any sort. His influence on the president's thinking, as well as Brennan's, became apparent in a bizarre press conference on August 1. "We tortured some folks," the president conceded—and then explained that there could be no possible legal accounting for these criminal acts, since the torturers were "real patriots."

Brennan meanwhile launched an extensive (and illegal) PR effort to defend those very same torturers. He coordinated his campaign with three former CIA directors who had managed the program—George Tenet, Porter Goss, and Michael Hayden—and tried to recruit a large number of CIA managers as well, most of whom refused to become involved. Marc Thiessen, a former Bush administration speechwriter, served as the group's publicist. For months before the release of the report, the CIA blitzed the American airwaves, disparaging the Senate's efforts and reminding viewers that "torture works." Even after the report came out, these same apologists continued to command far more time and attention on the nation's broadcast media than their critics. American journalists love a good story, after all. And many were still eager to build strong ties with the agency, whose continued ascent seemed assured, no matter how many lies and botched operations were revealed by the Senate probe.

This PR campaign did, however, suffer from one fatal flaw. As agency staffers and contractors prepared documents for the Senate committee, they also assembled a memorandum for CIA director Leon Panetta that summarized the same materials. This document, which has come to be called the Panetta Report, was accidentally transmitted by CIA staffers to the Senate investigators. Discovering their blooper, the CIA staffers then hacked into the Senate computers to take the report back—but the recipients, wary of just such chicanery, had already printed a copy and moved it to the secure document room in the Senate chambers. The Panetta Report had reached the same conclusions, on the basis of the same documents, as the Senate report. In other words, the CIA's own analysis and review of its records refuted all the cheerleading claims currently being trotted out by its cadre of publicists. Had the agency, in obstructing the report and spying on investigators, finally overplayed its hand? "Nothing could be further from the truth," insisted John Brennan, following in the footsteps of his predecessor Michael Hayden, whom the report depicts as a kind of unflappable Pinocchio, fibbing under oath at every opportunity.[8] With the report's publication, the CIA rushed out a web-based response, which was so riddled with demonstrable falsehoods that the agency was forced quietly to retract a good deal of it.

All of this begs the ultimate question of accountability. The issuance of the report devastated many of the carefully contrived denials of the CIA. But beyond embarrassment, have these disclosures led to accountability in any form? So far not even the figures who misled the congressional staff and attempted to obstruct their investigation have faced any form of accountability. On the other hand, the experience of Latin America is instructive in this regard. Practices like those used by the CIA were hidden, covered with national security classifications, and amnestied in Argentina, Chile, and Uruguay among other nations. It took a full generation— thirty years—before a formal process of accountability began to take hold, and octogenarian intelligence officers were dragged before courts and sent to prison. The predicate for any accountability in Latin America was a well-informed public that rejected the notion that torture of prisoners could ever be justified. Those who argue for accountability in America face a still steeper climb.

NOTES

1. Indeed, Bush was largely kept in the dark until 2006. On April 8 of that year, he was finally briefed by the CIA on its enhanced interrogation techniques. The report quotes from relevant CIA records, indicating that the president expressed some discomfort at the "image of a detainee, chained to the ceiling, clothed in a diaper, and forced to go to the bathroom on himself." [SICROT, 51].

2. SICROT, 9.

3. SICROT, 57.

4. SICROT, 293.

5. SICROT, 22.

6. SICROT, 141.

7. Embarrassed by the entire episode, the CIA surrendered their prisoner to Moammar Qaddafi's intelligence services, in whose custody he died mysteriously in 2009.

8. SICROT, 341–59.

ACKNOWLEDGMENTS

We would first like to acknowledge Alessandra Bastagli for recognizing the importance of this book and its helpful explanation of the Senate committee's complex depiction of the terrible anti-terror procedures utilized by the CIA. And, indeed, the incredible help of Katherine Haigler in its execution.

It was Bob Mecoy, our esteemed agent, who first thought of presenting our work to Nation Books, and we thank and applaud him for his insight.

None of this would have been accomplished without the help, for Ernie, of his wife Ruth, nor for Sid, without the support of his significant other, Audrey Hoffman.

Sid Jacobson and **Ernie Colón** first came together to create the *New York Times*-bestselling *The 9/11 Report: A Graphic Adaptation*. Since then, the pair have collaborated on graphic books about Che Guevara, the war on terror, and Anne Frank. Jacobson was formerly the managing editor and editor in chief of Harvey Comics and an executive editor at Marvel Comics. Artist Colón has worked at Harvey, Marvel, and DC Comics.

Jane Mayer is a staff writer for the *New Yorker* and the author of several bestselling and critically acclaimed narrative nonfiction books, including *The Dark Side* and *Dark Money*.

Scott Horton is a contributing editor at *Harper's* magazine and the author of *Lords of Secrecy*.

NATION
BOOKS

The Nation Institute

Nation.

Founded in 2000, **Nation Books** has become a leading voice in American independent publishing. The inspiration for the imprint came from the *Nation* magazine, the oldest independent and continuously published weekly magazine of politics and culture in the United States.

The imprint's mission is to produce authoritative books that break new ground and shed light on current social and political issues. We publish established authors who are leaders in their area of expertise, and endeavor to cultivate a new generation of emerging and talented writers. With each of our books we aim to positively affect cultural and political discourse.

Nation Books is a project of The Nation Institute, a nonprofit media center established to extend the reach of democratic ideals and strengthen the independent press. The Nation Institute is home to a dynamic range of programs: our award-winning Investigative Fund, which supports ground-breaking investigative journalism; the widely read and syndicated website TomDispatch; our internship program in conjunction with the *Nation* magazine; and Journalism Fellowships that fund up to 20 high-profile reporters every year.

For more information on Nation Books, the *Nation* magazine, and The Nation Institute, please visit:

www.nationbooks.org
www.nationinstitute.org
www.thenation.com
www.facebook.com/nationbooks.ny
Twitter: @nationbooks